CW01261341

The Pleasures of Queueing

a novel

Erik Martiny

Mastodon Publishing
Thoughts Made Real

All Rights Reserved

Printed in the United States of America

First Edition
1 2 3 4 5 6 7 8 9

This book is a work of fiction. Any references to historical events, real people, or real places are used fictitiously. Other names, characters, places, and events are products of the author's imagination, and any resemblance to actual events or places or persons, living or dead, is entirely coincidental.

Selections of up to one page may be reproduced without permission. To reproduce more than one page of any one portion of this book, write to C&R Press publishers John Gosslee and Andrew Sullivan.

Cover photography by Erik Martiny
Cover design: Mastadon Publishing
Interior design by Ali Chica
Cover photograph by Erik Martiny

Copyright ©2018 Erik Martiny

Library of Congress Cataloging-in-Publication Data

ISBN: 978-1-7320091-1-0
Library of Congress Control Number: 2018934094

Mastodon Publishing
Thoughts Made Real
mastodonpublishing.com

For special discounted bulk purchases, please contact:
Mastodon Publishing sales@mastodonpublishing.com
Contact info@mastodonpublishing.com to book events, readings and author signings.

Chapters

Franco-Irish Relations in 1971	8
I Sing of Olaf Glad and Big	19
Olafstein in Nutopia	24
There's a French Long-Wave Radio in Your Soul	30
Mrs. Cow's Crèche	37
Skin and Bones and Hair	45
Ireland and Hemorrhoids	51
The Expectant Bishop	57
Cheese and Choice	62
Cruelty® and Queueing	71
The Moon is Revealed	78
Doleo Ergo Sum	91
Merry Muck and Confirmation	97
Incest and School	105
The Year of the Flea	112
Shampoo, Love & Grease	121
Sartorius	130
The Perils of Comfort	135
I Get into College and then a Vagina	140

Wallflowers	150
Ars Amatoria	167
Annus Horribilis	177
Kleptomania and Urine	181
The Ship of Death	191

The Pleasures of Queueing

To all my loved ones

"A golden childhood is a bad preparation for adulthood."
Colette

"There are thousands of different kinds of families and each one is a small republic with its own laws and habits."
John McGahern

"The three essentials for an autobiography are that its author should have had an eccentric father, a miserable childhood and a hell of a time at his public school, but I have enjoyed none of these advantages. My father was as normal as rice pudding and my school years at Dulwich were just six years of unbroken bliss."
P. G. Wodehouse

Disclaimer:
The characters in this novel are entirely fictitious. Any persons resembling them should consider fleeing to Brazil.

1
Franco-Irish Relations in 1971

The USA, the USSR and France test nuclear missiles. Apollo 14 returns to Earth. Charles Manson is convicted of murder. Richard Nixon installs a secret taping system in the White House.

About 200,000 anti-Vietnam War protesters march on Washington. The US and Japan sign an agreement to return Okinawa to Japan. The British begin internment without trial in Northern Ireland. Nikita Khrushchev is buried in Moscow. John Lennon sings "Imagine." Soviet Mars 2 becomes the first spacecraft to crash land on Mars. *A Clockwork Orange* opens in cinemas. Swiss men accept female suffrage. Woody Allen releases *Bananas*.

I am conceived in the missionary position, on a sixty-year-old, British-made Irish heirloom mattress, after three hours in the prolonged plateau phase, one of the crucially defining features of *coitus reservatus*. Reluctantly forsaking the only accommodation I am to have entirely to myself for the next 24 years, my body is extruded from the amniotic luxury of my mother's womb. I am left holding the placenta against my chest like a deflated Gaelic football.

My mother, exhausted by the death of Nikita Khrushchev, the conviction of Charles Manson, the hidden tinkering of Richard Nixon under the table and giving birth, bleeds for 35 hours, adopts the complexion and texture of a white mushroom, tells my father that she feels like the flower of death in a field of green snow, but recovers three days later.

Unlike most kids born in Cork, I am not born in the hospital known as "de Bonz", the Irish contraction of The Bon Secours Maternity Hospital. For my mother, this colloquialism evokes "the bombs" or some unpleasant form of torture in favour with the IRA such as kneecapping or fingernail extraction, or the removal of bones as in "spill de fuckin beans or we'll take yer fuckin bonz out." Although it is a private hospital and therefore somewhat select, she dislikes the name of the place and will have nothing to do with it.

In early summer, my parents leave the more eloquently-named Erinville Hospital and return to Bishopstown Drive where they have built something of a human-sized nest for the family on the outskirts of the block, having gathered together the fluffiest meter-long feathers fallen from the wings of Stephen Dedalus on his ascent towards the sun-pierced, marshmallow clouds.

In less surreal, more down-to-earth terms, what we have is the first eco-friendly, recycled-product habitation in the otherwise semi-detached concrete suburbs of Cork. To confect this New Age house-nest on the outskirts of Bishopstown, my parents have gone to great lengths.

Having anticipated the principle of nothing gets lost, everything can be recycled, they make use of intertwined branches (hand-picked in the woods), and knot them together with disused clothes found in junk yards and various junk gardens spread out around the city. Uncoiled shopping trolleys have been rewelded into web-like, wall-supporting shapes. Insulation has been provided by stacked-up bound clods of Seamus Heaney Heritage Peat™, ribbed and strengthened by the tannin-preserved bones of prehistoric men, women and children. Plastic cider bottles stuffed with shopping bags serve as bisque-colored, soft-cornered, extra-insulating bricks.

From the outside, however, our house looks surprisingly similar to the other houses in the estate. My parents have conceded that a degree of camouflage is essential for their children's cultural and psychological integration. Coated in a splattering of whitewash and lumpy, porridge-like, pebble-thickened sizing, the house almost blends in with the others.

On close inspection, however, it still looks rough and ready enough to put off even the most enthusiastic of thieves. My father even scatters a few worm-eaten planks around the front garden to make the place look run-down and worthless in case inexperienced burglars mistake the eco-hovel for a well-to-do residence simply because it is situated in a fairly affluent area. The strategy works wonders, protecting us from intrusion. To my knowledge, every other house in the vicinity gets burgled except ours.

Meanwhile, back in 1971, my convalescing mother is cozily installed in bed, enthroned in soft puffy pillows that buttress her back and nestle her throbbing, thistle-thatched perineum. My father brings her up a cup of warm pre-Chernobyl milk laced with honey, a sprinkling of cocoa, and cinnamon.

There she sits, completely appeased, taking sips of warm liquid cow, watching the baby attempt facial expressions. Her name is Anne Montcocq, née Áine O'Neill. She has the slightly elfin features that - in my relatively limited geographical experience - can be found among certain Irish, Swedish, Polish and Japanese women. Her smile is full of small, soft-looking teeth spiked with a single snaggled, briefly vampiric prolongation that will keep me enthralled in decades to come each time I encounter the feature in another woman's mouth.

Anne Montcocq is a woman of character who rarely fails to subdue her husband and the twenty-seven children to which she will eventually give birth. She has the weight of tradition to back up her will.

Look up an image of the Danish actress Anna Karina dressed as a nun in Jacques Rivette's *La Religieuse* (1966) on Youtube.com and you'll have an inkling of what Anne Montcocq looks like at this point in her life.

In fact for some unexplained reason that will remain unexplained, Anna Karina and Anne Montcocq are doubles that have taken largely divergent paths. They were born the same day (22 September 1940) and look like identical twins. The only difference between my mother and La Religieuse is that Anne Montcocq is in the end no rebel to ecclesiastical indoctrination. On the contrary. She is about as church-abiding as it's possible to be. A true-blue, dyed-in-the-wool, out-and-out, die-hard Holy Mary.

Anne is sensitive to the refinements of high art but she is also an undiscriminating sucker for artistically stale, churchy-kitshy iconography. She accumulates holy books by the gross, hundreds of bookmarks, thousands of images. She has the behavior of a Catholic iconophile after the Council of Trent.

Pious pictures and religious knick-knacks of all sizes and shapes lie scattered around the house, standing on shelves, window-sills and radiators, sticking out of books, nooks, crannies, cracks in the kitchen, the living room, the bathroom, the toilet. We have scaled-down, home entertainment versions of the Wailing Wall in each room. My father dismissively calls her church trinkets *bondieuseries*, which in English literally translated means 'goodgoderies'.

Anne Montcocq follows scripture down to a T. She kowtows to priests, goes to mass three times on week days, twice on Sunday. Mercifully, at this early stage in my life, I do not yet know that I will have Mass coming out of my ears, that there will be Mass growing off the stumps of trees in our garden.

Anne confesses everything to the parish priest. Although the edicts of Vatican II are successfully adopted in Ireland, officially doing away with Latin as the only admissible liturgical language, my mother insists on conducting her confessions in the ancient idiom for its ceremonial allure and because it provides concealment of sins she is compelled to commit in the bonds of matrimony behind a veil of gentility, a veneer of Augustinian prestige.

Her Latin confessions include words - my father later tells me - like *fellatio ad patrem, cunnilingus ad mater, coitus interruptus frequentus, coitus reservatus ad nauseam*. Her Latin is sometimes faulty. Like Shakespeare before her, she has little Latin and less Gaelic, despite her fervent, militant Irishness.

Anne Montcocq would drink nothing but bottled holy water if she could get her hands on enough of it. If she could have the priest consecrate the water reservoirs of the city, including the sewage system, she would have it be so.

From a secular perspective, my mother's main redeeming feature is the almost unreserved pagan relish she has for sexual intercourse. Only with my father, needless to say.

By contrast, Martin Montcocq is almost everything my mother is not. He is French to the tips of his far-reaching, sensual French toes and remains decidedly French despite the 33 years he spends in Ireland under professional duress.

His choice of bride (and Anne's choice of husband) is a mystery to everyone who knows them. He later tells me that Áine O'Neill was the only attractive woman who denied him "vaginal access" before marriage and that this was one of the factors that riled him into marrying her so that he could come and go "within the liquid silk of your mother's lovely labia."

Believe it or not, this is actually the way Martin Montcocq speaks, even to his own children, as soon as we are able to understand his vocabulary and even before.

As you will see in the course of this story if you have not been deterred by its non-PC off-color quality so far, my father has a strangely distanced way of expressing what he means. As the first offspring to spring from Martin Montcocq's old-fashioned loins, I inherit something of his linguistic manner after so many years of being subjected to his words and his sometimes convoluted syntax. What Martin calls his "sesquipedalian lexis" in both French and English will make him unpopular at work and habitually incomprehensible at home. You may be unsurprised to learn that Martin Montcocq is Modern Poetry Professor at University College Cork, specialized in the impact of Stéphane Mallarmé on Anglo-Irish literature since Joyce.

But first let us linger a little longer on the subject of my father's libidinal proclivities. They have a sizeable impact on the development of my life and the evolution of the household and require some attention for things to be clear.

Martin Montcocq is not just a Frenchman; he is a Frenchman of archetypal proportions. A Frenchman who came of age during the sexual revolt of the sixties. You might say that before the advent of my father, Vatican II is as close as Ireland gets to any kind of social revolution at this time. There are no hippies to be seen in Cork and you have to go as far afield as London to spot anything as exotic as flamingoes or spikey, pink-and-orange-haired punks.

Although official historians have neglected this fact, Martin Montcocq's presence brings Ireland a significant, if localized, step closer to experiencing the ripples of the international student revolt of 1968.

My father is in himself a kind of hippy experiment, and for good or for bad, our home becomes his makeshift laboratory. Think of the Montcocq household as a microcosm of what might have happened to Ireland if the Parisian spirit of 1968 had been allowed to blow upon it and you will have a fairly good idea of what it was like to grow up in its laboratory.

1968, I should say, and the shadow of World War II. As you will see later, my father's personality is a brace of warring paradoxes.

Before he meets my mother, Martin claims to have probed "the consenting vaginas" of no less than 431 women and 56 men of all nationalities, having manifested a marked relish for Swedish, American and Italian orifices.

Although my father speaks to me in this crudely objectifying way - that is strangely a little euphuistic at the same time - his former Scandinavian paramours have made him highly receptive to the aspirations of the Feminist Movement. He displays remarkably few macho features and is always careful to encourage the women he knows, as well as those he does not know when he hears them speak on the radio.

As you can see, the behavioral revolution of the Sixties has hit my father hard and it is only thanks to my mother and her initial genital reticence that Martin Montcocq becomes a faithful husband, an unflaggingly attentive father who survives the AIDS epidemic and other venereal complications.

Too little has been said of the heroism of the ordinary man who manages to remain faithful for years, sometimes decades, to the same woman when everything in his body is scientifically screaming for him to procreate and multiply with every available adult female, and the underage, unavailable ones too.

Before you brush this heroism bit off as typical male talk, consider the fact that from the age of 15, the body of the average human male is flooded with two full gallons of testosterone a day, which means that an unmanageable, overpoweringly strong chemical inflow is making you sexually saturated, libidinally loaded, before you are even able to climb out of bed and lever your erection into a mercifully elastic pair of modern underpants. I challenge any woman to avoid getting that glazed-eye look every ten seconds in a crowded street on a hot summer afternoon, never mind staying faithful for life, with that amount of inebriating chemicals coursing through every vein, popping and fizzing in every cell of her body.

Ok, it's true that when the human female is pregnant she emits pheromones that trigger prolactin production in the male, making his testosterone drop by a merciful 30%. But still, think about it for a second. We are talking about having to battle off 70% of two gallons a day up to the endlessly-deferred relief of the god-given andropause.

You could say that although my mother's obstetric and educational heroism is blatant everywhere in this story, the other main hero of this book is therefore my father who not only has to contend with the average male compulsion to breed with every woman in sight: Martin Montcocq later tells me that he is afflicted with satyriasis - the mythological term for hypersexuality.

To put it politely, this means that spermatozoa are practically oozing out of poor Martin's ears. At this stage in his life, my father would probably break the Guinness Record for the hardiest, speediest, most energy-driven, longest-jumping spermatozoon in history. We're talking about sperm swimming faster than a horde of voracious, ocean-crossing mammals.

Perhaps you are wondering how a man afflicted with satyriasis can form a viable couple with an ultra-orthodox Catholic. What happens when two such opposites meet? The answer - a noticeable increase in the Irish population - is one of the foremost subjects of this memoir.

This being said, if this is a story of bohemia and bountiful procreation, as I suggested before, you will find that it is also something of a postwar novel.

It's usually easy enough to date the end of a war, give or take a month or two, the notion of a world war as a moveable feast, depending on the country, etcetera, but the question to ask is where do you situate the end of the postwar?

Do you consider the postwar era over when the last bomb-shelled building has been replaced or restored? Does the postwar period end when the last Auschwitz survivor succumbs, when the last Central European country manages to haul its average citizen above the poverty line?

Our father keeps a row of polished brass bomb shells in the sitting room and the hall. Granted, our mother uses them to pot plants, but they are still there every day of our childhood, looming like long, mirror-like, gold-colored urns, pervading their funerary atmosphere. Martin has inherited them from his father who was a French officer in the war so they are sacred, and not to be touched.

On festive days, Martin takes out a candlestick that is actually the butt of an unidentifiable metallic object whose nature remains mysteriously indeterminate. It has the weight of almost a kilo and a chamber at the bottom that can't be pried open. Martin says it could be the bottom of a small missile or even an antiquated cylindrical grenade. It's a mystery to him too.

When some of us later complain that it might possibly be dangerous, he cries out in indignation and scorn, saying how silly, it couldn't possibly explode thirty years after the war. He lights up the candle and we sing. But enough of war and its aftermaths for the time being. Let us return for a moment to the baby, as I'm sure you've forgotten it by now.

Can you hear it howling in distress from upstairs? Anne Montcocq's breasts have failed to release their expected discharge. While most women's breasts leak creamy colostrum even before giving birth, Anne's bosoms have remained as dry as beached jellyfish.

The baby is screaming so much its tongue is flapping like the accelerating clapper of a mouth-bell.

Martin Montcocq himself tries sucking a little milk from the 20 lactiferous ducts that perforate his wife's nipples, but succeeds only in bruising poor Anne's papillae.

As a staunch supporter of the superior properties of colostrum, Anne is now ready to sweat milk through the pores of her fingers, develop supernumerary nipples, before she will give in to Martin's supplications regarding the usefulness of rehydrated powder milk dispensed from a bottle.

It is therefore only far into the night that the long-awaited milk is finally expelled into the groaning mouth of the baby. It sucks for almost an hour, then collapses into Anne's hands in open-mouthed bliss and exhaustion.

Nine days later, the baby is doing well and Martin is sent out to register the names they have chosen to bestow. After lengthy discussions, they settle on a name that neither of them really likes, but it is the only one they both agree is reasonably pleasant to hear.

Little does the baby know that as it gurgles happily and practices smiling muscles with magic mother, Martin Montcocq is having second thoughts on his way to the Office of Vital Records.

Martin is entertaining the thought of slipping in his own preference instead.

Unsurprisingly, Anne has favored names like Andrew, David, Liam and Samson. For the most eccentric reasons, Martin has a liking for names that smack of Viking gods and Danish Existentialists. As he stops in front of the Registrar's Office, he is still debating the merits of names like Odin, Thorsten, Baldr, Vili, Vali and Vé.

He hesitates and enters the Registrar's and when he is given the file to fill in at the desk, he hesitates again, as if he is about to give a baby bull a *coup de grâce*, the final thrust with his pen.

On the form he writes   OLAF   SØREN   Montcocq.

Martin is a little irritable this morning, partially because he has been disturbed by the baby's scream-filled sleep, and partially because he feels neglected by his wife since the baby is out of her uterus. He feels he deserves to have his way in this important matter, so the baby's fate is sealed. Olaf it is to be because Martin's favorite Swedish politician is Olof Palme and e e cummings wrote a stirring poem in 1931, about "Olaf glad and big", a conscientious objector who refuses to kiss the flag, is tortured and thrown in a dungeon to die.

Time goes by, Anne forgives Martin his wayward moment and, for better or for worse, mostly worse, I am saddled with Olaf for life.

My first memory serves as an indicator of what awaits me under the unfortunate cognomen. I am fattening nicely under the mammary ministrations of mother when one day, as my father puts it in his nineteenth-century Edgar Allen Poe style, "paradise is purloined".

The golden milk, the mellifluous miracle, the gorgeous milk of human kindness goes sour.

No doubt because I have been sucking so hard on Anne's overtaxed papillae, one of them, and then the other, contracts an infection and I begin to feel increasing amounts of pus mixed in with my ambrosia.

The infection begins to spread and is now purulent beyond acceptance, especially by the standards of a baby. I sputter, cough and refuse to take the now dreadful pus-dispenser in my mouth. This incites Anne to shout for the very first time in her career as a mother. She stuffs the nefarious nipple into my averted battling mouth.

Martin pleads with her to give up breast-feeding but Anne refuses to give in. It has become a point of honor and she treats me as if I am a brazen child refusing to chew his meat on a whim.

It is the only moment in which Anne behaves out of character. She is otherwise always gentle, always caring and steadfast, even heroic in putting up with a queer fish of a husband and the swarm of children to which she will give birth.

After much anguished wrenching and stuffing, prodding and pronging, Anne Montcocq succumbs in religious despair to the necessary evil of cow milk in a baby bottle and I am able to swallow again without septic fluid squirting against my taste buds.

But as soon as the breast infection disappears, baby bottle, bottle brush, sterilizer and milk powder are all thrown by the wayside. Anne Montcocq rightly reasserts the importance of receiving maternal antibodies straight from the nipple.

She may be a traditional Holy Mary, my mother nevertheless becomes my first alt-feminist icon, imprinting forever in my mind the wonderful primacy of women. Despite her flaws, Anne Montcocq's inspirational leadership causes me to become a female supremacist at a very early age. It is only after experiencing a series of surprisingly complex girlfriends in my late teens that I renounce the doctrine of female superiority and become a staunch egalitarian.

Three members of the IRA are killed when a bomb they are carrying explodes in County Derry. The Socialist Party of Ireland is formed in Dublin. The United Kingdom gives up its military bases in Malta. Khmer Rouge rebels intensify assaults on Cambodian government positions. India launches a massive invasion of East Pakistan. *Diamonds Are Forever* is released. Ewan McGregor, Mark Wahlberg, Snoop Dogg, Winona Ryder are born. Coco Chanel, Igor Stravinsky and Louis Armstrong depart.

2
I Sing of Olaf Glad and Big

A one-million-kilo meteorite grazes the atmosphere above Canada. People standing on top of skyscrapers in Toronto say they feel the warmth of its passing. A notable upsurge in public morale is noted by many and lovemaking increases exponentially for the next three days in the public toilets of Swedish train stations, museums in Paris, telephone booths in Cap d'Ail, dog kennels in Cork, shop windows in Liège, trees in Silvershum, Cathedrals in Oxfordshire.

On Bloody Sunday, British soldiers shoot 13 Irish Catholics in (London) Derry. Thomas Kinsella writes the poem "Butcher's Dozen." A bootlegger in New Delhi sells wood alcohol to a wedding party killing 100. The stewardess Vesna Vulovic survives a 10,160m fall without a parachute.

The baby who is one of the hapless subjects of this book survives a 1,20m fall after having wobbled and tripped over its feet. It happens during the period in which Martin Montcocq, prouder than ever, refers to the recently mobile toddler as "the pedestrian baby."

Unfortunately for the walking baby, he falls against the edge of a door jamb at the considerable speed of 33.2 kilometers an hour, which has the effect of slicing through the milk-soft skin of his cranium and parting the still tender fibers of the skull to within half a millimeter of the brain.

Rushing to the fallen baby, Martin closes his hand around the no longer walking baby's blood-dribbling forehead, feeling like he has suddenly been cast six years into the future onto the film set of *The Deer Hunter*. For a freakish premonitory instant, he experiences what it is like to be Robert De Niro attempting to contain the bullet wound in Christopher Walken's oozing head.

At the hospital, the nurse stares at the baby as if she is an extra in a silent horror film and rushes off to get a doctor. Strangely enough, the toddler seems fine, starts lounging around again as if everything's hunky dory. A turbaned Pakistani Muslim sitting next to them in the waiting room peers closely into the wound, raises wide-open eyes to Martin and Anne, and says "Jesus."

Anne is sitting on her chair looking whiter than white. Martin walks behind the indefatigable unsteadily roving toddler, ready to pounce at every wobble.

Twenty interminable minutes later, a doctor calls them in, sews up the skin on the cranium with a long trembling needle and tells them that the skull will probably mend itself without assistance. When asked about potential brain damage, she pretends not to hear. They are to contact her immediately if the child shows signs of weakness, vomiting, over-sleeping or any sort of impairment.

The stitched aperture in Baby Frankenstein's forehead eventually heals, leaving behind it a pale moon crescent scar. Martin calls his son "the man from the moon." It is a sweet name but it fails to stop the walking baby from falling. From then onwards, Olafstein stumbles over its feet, trips over toys, gets its toes caught in rugs, cushions, wires, floorboards, fireplace settings, falling invariably head first, head-butting every fixture, every object in sight. It even falls from its bed, its rocking-horse, its fire-engine, its truck. In heart-stopping, almost funereal silence, Martin even witnesses it keeling over with a massive, heart-chilling thud straight onto its forehead from a sitting position and then lying motionless.

Olafstein falls so many times onto his freshly stitched wound that the scar tissue on his brow dilates into a fuzzy, pus-oozing wax moon that sports most of the colors of the rainbow.

In the evening, Martin Montcocq lectures his wife.

"Thank Darwin that the forehead is thicker than other parts of the skull. Early head-butting must have prompted nature to fortify the forehead. We should really be called something like *Pachycephalosapiens* - thick-headed knowers - beings who have been able to remain semi-clever despite incessant insults to the brain. If you look at other baby mammals, they slip and fall a little in the first few minutes of their lives. Biped human mammals keel over repeatedly for the first four years of their lives probably causing untold damage to the mind, despite the reinforced forehead. I'm sure it's why we're such self-destructive, pathologically domineering, mentally defective, war-mongering savages."

Anne Montcocq nods sadly in silence.

After two years, Olafstein's brain has been sufficiently damaged and his body moves onto other things like using imbalance to master the locomotive technique known as running. But when at the end of the year Little Man in the Moon shows no signs of improved stability, Anne goes to consult a neurologist.

The specialist explains that she need not worry inordinately about the near future as the worst form of damage is done in the first nine months after birth. In the early stages, he adds, the brain has not yet filled the cranial cavity and thus floats about like a rubber duck in a bathtub. Every time the head is hit or shaken even a little, the brain is projected at full speed against the roof of the skull causing occasionally permanent fissures and internal bruising. At best, this leads to imperfect balance and attention deficit. In worst case scenarios, it causes personality disorders and/or death.

The neurologist asks if the baby has ever been shaken in a fit of anger as an infant.

"Was he ever excessively dandled?"

"Dandled?"

"You know, bounced up and down on the knee, that sort of thing."

Anne thinks back and pronounces a hesitant "no", but then she remembers something else.

She takes her leave of the doctor and goes home. When she tells Martin about dandling and baby tossing, he goes pale, lets out a long portentous sigh, and looking at the ceiling says *"Putain de merde de bordel de Dieu"* (which literally translated means "Hooker of shit of the whorehouse of God" – which in the mouth of a Frenchman expresses a high degree of discomposure).

Anne doesn't usually react to her husband's blasphemous, potentially sexist pronouncements, but this one sours her mood for the rest of the morning.

They look at each other and think about how in their joy at having a child they swing-dance and dandle and throw Olaf in the air. "A kind of criminal joy", Martin reflects, as he remembers pitching the baby high above his arms and the one time its head even banged off the ceiling, probably sustaining untold internal damage on its way down to his arms.

Martin vows he will spend the rest of his free time acting as Olafstein's bodyguard. He covers the surface of every room with thick-piled wall-to-wall carpet, not realizing that this will later cause Olafstein to endure 20 years of acarid-related asthma, but as they say, the road to hell is paved with good intentions.

Even the walls of Olafstein's room are covered in meter-high paisley carpeting. All objects are systematically removed from the ground, wires cellotaped back to the wainscoting, doors left open all day long so that nothing can come in the way of the wobbling boy. When Martin is in charge of minding Olafstein, his heart jumps every time the child gets up or leaves the room. He barks "careful!" twice a minute and has to pounce to adjust the little boy's gait. Each additional knock to Olafstein's head sends a resounding echo through Martin's battered heart.

The problem persists for another two years and then starts to disappear.

"IQ is not generally impaired in these cases", the neurologist says, "but it is more than likely that he will suffer from attention deficit and possibly some psychotic episodes, especially in his teens. He will most likely have difficulty reading and linking letters to sounds and the act of writing a novel will require him to ingurgitate inordinate quantities of coffee."

Left to his own devices outside in the garden, Olafstein pulls the green hair off the ground, peers into holes, wedges his nails into cracks, picks up slugs, squashes one to a pulp in his fist and stuffs the remains for safekeeping in his pocket. In the fields, the cow pats sleep on the dark wet green hair. He imagines cow poo falling into milk that is bottled and delivered to someone's front door.

The blackberries on the blackberry bush burst their blood over his fingers. On the white garden walls and the squarely capped pillars, tiny red spiders crawl and scamper up his hands. He watches the blood-spiders have the run of his arms.

A herd of stampeding elephants kills 24 people in Chandka Forest, India. The first female rabbi is appointed in America. The first two women begin training as FBI agents. The first Gay Pride march takes place in England. David Bowie releases *Rise & Fall of Ziggy Stardust*. John Lennon says his phone is being tapped by the FBI.

On Bloody Friday, 22 IRA bombs explode in Belfast. The last American ground troops leave Vietnam. 11 Israeli athletes are murdered at the Munich Olympics. Chuck Berry's "My Ding-a-ling" is Number One in the charts. Credit cards are introduced in Great Britain. Amanda Peet, Jennifer Garner, Zinedine Zidane, Ben Affleck, Cameron Diaz, Gwyneth Paltrow and Jude Law are born. J. Edgar Hoover, Ezra Pound and Harry Truman come to naught.

3
Olafstein in Nutopia

President Nixon signs the Endangered Species Act into law. Paul and Linda McCartney are fined £100 for growing cannabis at home. Nixon authorizes the construction of the Alaskan pipeline. Veronica Lake dies before Olafstein has time to consider the notion of sexual orientation. John Lennon and Yoko Ono form a new country called Nutopia with no laws or boundaries. Its national anthem is silence.

Olafstein's teething and colic pains are added to the throbbing of his head wounds. His lamentations fill the house like the jeremiads of Jeremiah. An endless wail that pierces Martin's chest like a corkscrew, finding its way into Anne's facial muscles and the twitches in her fingers.

Aspirin is too strong for Olafstein sad and small so Anne and Martin have to massage the little boy's gums with a home-made paste that alleviates little, if anything, but affords them both a feeling that something useful is being done.

Then finally the moaning ceases and the Nutopian silence left in its wake is pure bliss. Twenty-four karat silence, silence that surpasses the purest notes on the inaudible scale of the music of the spheres.

Into this diamond of soundlessness and the end of pain, a sense of enduring consciousness dawns on me. A million memory cells burst into life, healing some of the breaches in my badly knocked brain.

The next day, when my father is off to University on his old high nelly of a bike and my mother has slipped out to see a neighbor, I begin to explore the kitchen bric-a-brac heaped up in the cupboards. I trip over my feet, wham my head on the thick rubber linoleum and then put out my arms. There's a crescent-shaped pus-and-blood stain on the floor. An average fall, no major harm done, just a little bit dazed. I get up, totter anew, almost smack my skull into the pointy edge of the table but manage to hold onto a chair just in time.

The cupboard between the dishwasher and the wall contains a thousand plastic bags of every color and size, enough to choke all the turtles and tortoises of the Galapagos Islands and a hundred toddlers to boot.

I am not yet interested in putting my head experimentally into hermetic plastic bags and getting tangled in knots. But I am still more than anything a sensualist so I plunge my arm into the crinkly mass of bags, exploring the labyrinth of densely-packed, multi-layered plastic.

I open another creaky cupboard to find sponges by the dozen, shreds of scouring metal mesh, moldering rags, festering tea-towels and filth-stained floor cloths. Dirt is not something that repels me, on the contrary. At this point in my existence, I have already tasted the contents of two heavily-soiled nappies to my parents' utter dismay, my mother practically fainting with disgust, my father regretting the now less than delicious memory of the kisses he gave me on those chocolaty-looking streaks on my cheeks.

But today it is not towards excrement-tasting that I am drawn, nor to the pleasures of slime-fingering or snot-sampling, but to the ultra-toxic delights that I come upon in one of the cupboards, a stiff one with a loosened safety catch that I easily yank open.

I stand before the deadly cupboard, smiling with the appetite of a mad scientist. I shaky-shake a few almost empty bottles. Two of them have a big black X at the back. One of them is full to the brim with syrupy, delicious-looking purple, but the most dazzling of all is a hefty cardboard box that contains tiny white particles like sugar only more powerfully white. I chew the cardboard a little and then stick my mouth, nose and tongue in the lovely pure powder.

Not as good as sugar by a long shot. I spit and try to wipe the stuff off my tongue. This is no good as food but I can still use it. I take the big box outside and there I find the gutter exactly where I left it the day before. I spill a good bit of the powder into the hole.

I go and find a stick and stir down the beautiful mucky mixture until the puddle in the gutter has turned lovely light brown. I pour, pour the powder until the whole box is empty and a floating hill of white stuff emerges from the puddle. I stir the stuff back in, making beige lumpy porridge.

I take a handful of chunky-goo and walk around the garden looking for the right target, and there, hanging from the clothes line, are the billowing white sheets that mommy hangs out to dry.

It's just what I'm looking for, but my aim isn't good.

I go back with another handful, get up closer this time, fling the filth right on target and finger it into streaks along the lovely white sheets.

This is really, really good fun. I like this a lot. This game is pure me. It is funny, good and interesting.

But then I hear a scream from inside the house and mommy runs out. I am man-handled to the sink and washed in icy-cold water, brimming with glee.

Time passes, and then I notice one day in my parents' bed how my mother's belly has grown round and hard as a very big ball. I whack the belly with my hand. No! she says. I ask her why she is so fat and she says I'm going to have a baby brother, or maybe a sister. What is that, I ask, and she says it is a little person like you only smaller like a doll or a teddy bear and you will have to be a good brother and protect the baby and not be jealous because mummy loves you and daddy loves you too.

I take this in, not really believing that you can have a whole person, or even a doll, in your belly. How did a sister or a brother get there in the first place and why is he hiding curled up like a hedgehog under her nightie? She makes me put my ear to her belly the way we've listened to the sound of the sea in a shell at the beach. All I can hear is my own ear rubbing against her nightie, but then she pulls it up and places my head on the over-stretched skin of her belly and I hear a fizz and a gurgle.

The baby turns out to be two babies later, a thing they call Twins, two little sisters instead of the brother I have been setting my sights on. But they are funny, with their Mister Magoo faces and their wee-spouting folds. We laugh a lot one day, the three of us together when one of them, the one called Deirdre, lets loose a jet-propelled fart while mommy is changing her nappy.

Daddy proclaims that Deirdre has "a nuclear-powered bottom." He winks at me and explains "the hammer of Thor in her bowels." I know what he means. He has been reading me a book called *Scandinavian Legends*.

Mommy is exclaiming proudly that she has been fleet of foot, quick enough to get out of the way a split second before the bottom explodes across the room. She realizes by the look on our faces that at least half of it is splattered over her shirt and her skirt.

Martin Montcocq, in true French scatological spirit, gets out his measuring tape to register a new record. He calls his parents up in France on the spot to boast about Deirdre's phenomenal energy.

"*Ce sera une musicienne !*"

He always yells into the telephone so that the sound can cover the distance all the way to France.

Another day it is the other twin, the one my father has again managed to name according to his interests in all things Nordic. She is called Sif, who is supposed to be Thor's wife, or something.

Anyway, one day my father is holding Sif aloft after having released her from her chocolate-colored nappy. He is holding her up in the air by the armpits not quite knowing what to do because the nappy is soiled, the baby's back is carpeted in a thick layer of feces and my mother is ferreting for cotton in the drawers.

Suddenly, to complicate matters, Sif starts to wee. A strong jet of pee spouts onto the carpet, then the bed. My father's misguided reflex is to swing abruptly around, away from the bed. Looking at the ground to see if the faux-Persian rug hasn't been damaged, he realizes in horror that he has been holding Sif over the desk.

She has just copiously sprayed a large pile of uncorrected student essays.

After a lot of shouting and recriminating, Martin tells Anne that as far as he can see, he is left with two options. He can tell his students he has lost their essays - but that doesn't seem plausible and wouldn't go down well with the Acting Head, who is usually a bit of an acting Dick Head - or he can attempt to dry them with a hairdryer and hope the smell will evaporate in a week.

He tries drying the Victorian poetry essays but after a few days the smell is still there, faint but persistent, and he can hardly see himself being accused of urinating on his students' end of term assessments. So finally, with a strong measure of relief, he decides to photocopy the smell off the paper.

When he hands the photocopied essays back — having burnt the originals in case he is asked to hand them in - he tries to keep a straight face in the lecture hall and announces on the microphone that there was a little mishap with a teapot so he had to resort to a way of giving back the papers in some presentable form.

Ireland is still a fuggy, straitlaced place in the early 1970s and kissing students, lolling in abandon on the grass squares in front of the west wing of University College Cork, have not appeared yet, despite photographic proof provided by *Le baiser de l'hôtel de ville* which shows it can be done.

Pub-crawl vomit trails have yet to be seen along the footpaths in large quantities, so pissing on your students' essays is not a thing to be laughed at. Not fully realizing that in the social sphere he inhabits it is an almost punishable incident, my father discloses the funny secret to a colleague who greets the story in silence. Two days later, my father's lecture is almost empty and the few students who have turned up avoid looking him in the eye.

Meanwhile, I have been learning to count to a 100. I count, count and count. I count until it feels I am reaching into space, creating matter itself. Counting is pure exhilaration. I am creating the Universe, expanding its confines, counting the world into existence.

Stevie Wonder goes into a four-day coma. The first portable cell phone call is made in New York. Greece chooses to be a republic rather than a monarchy. A US psychiatrist says that homosexuals are not mentally ill. Egypt and Israel exchange prisoners of war.

The Italian Fascist organization Ordine Nuovo is disbanded. The Sydney Opera House and Bosphorus bridge are opened. Adrien Brody and Kate Beckinsale warm to life. Lyndon Johnson, Pablo Picasso, Noël Coward, J.R.R Tolkien and Bruce Lee cool off.

4
There's a French Long-Wave Radio Station in Your Soul

The worst fire in Argentine history destroys over a million acres. Nixon refuses to hand over tapes to the Watergate Committee. England begins a three-day working week during a mine strike. The Dutch speed limit is set at 100km due to the oil crisis. Iran/Iraqi border fighting breaks out. The dissident writer Alexander Solzhenitsyn is expelled from the USSR.

The last Japanese soldier, a guerrilla operating in the Philippines, surrenders, 29 years after World War II ends. Most Arab oil-producing nations discontinue their embargo against the US. An attempt is made to kidnap Princess Anne in London's Pall Mall. Ayatollah Khomeini calls for an Islamic Republic.

You have probably stopped wondering at this stage why each chapter of this memoir-novel begins and ends with a summary of the world news highlights of the year. In all probability, you will have interpreted it as a postmodernist whim, a contextualizing device, self-aggrandizement, a self-belittling statement of relativity, or the author trying to look globally committed, politically and historically aware in an *engagé* sort of way.

Oh, sweet astute reader, you are not entirely wrong in assuming all of this and yet there is a sense in which I am more than figuratively plugged in as a member of the Montcocq household. The short French news bulletins provided in translation are in fact condensed samples of the informative noise pollution that pervades our house in Bishoptown, County Cork, Ireland.

Like a lot of expatriate Frenchmen, our father never ceases to be French. The nub of him, all the spokes of him, remain entirely Franco-foreign. Despite spending 33 years on Irish soil, he does not assimilate, wipe away or dilute his Frenchness over time. As a true blue, white and red *homo gallicus*, there is something within him that refuses to don the camouflaging colors of *homo hibernicus*.

The notion of the melting pot is inconceivable to Martin Montcocq. At a time when Afro-European authors are proclaiming their Negritude, my father holds on tight to his Frenchitude like Lady Liberty holding the flame of freedom aloft to the Atlantic. He informs us more than once that the Statue of Liberty was created by a Frenchman and that if he had anything to do with it the monumental sculpture would have stayed where it belonged as one of the urban mounts of Paris. The Statue of Liberty is in fact a Frenchwoman exiled in Alien America proclaiming her refusal to melt in the pot.

Although he does have a certain amount of interaction with the local Irish population, Martin Montcocq prides himself on remaining as French as it's possible to be, despite the constraints imposed by semi-voluntary expatriation.

Frenchitudinists like my father hanker to embrace the mother country all the more so because they feel painfully cut off from it. They do not wish to entertain the notion of a hybrid or hyphenated identity. Not once in several decades does Martin Montcocq allow his accent to adopt the rhythms and sounds of Anglo-Irish speech. He is adamant about being called Martin with a stress on the second syllable rather than the first, with a nasal vocalization of the ending, and the uvular rolling of the r, which to an Anglophone is akin to something like *Marrr* (guttural choking sound) *hh* (spitting sound) *tain*! He also requires friends and neighbors to pronounce our family name the way it's pronounced in French. People have been debarred from friendship because of their inability or unwillingness to comply with this simple request.

In his presence, English is strictly off-limits. Even Anne Montcocq shies away from addressing her husband in English at home. If our conversation degenerates into Hiberno-English (which it invariably does when we are left to ourselves), we quickly learn to code-switch to French as soon as Martin is within ear-shot.

It's usually not a good idea to be caught speaking television-inspired Hiberno-American either in the vicinity of Papa-Professor Montcocq. So, if in the course of this novel you begin to wonder why the dialogue switches from English to French, it is not just because the language centers of our brains are as fickle and random as a badly tuned radio, it is because at least one of us has registered the proximity of Father.

Because Father French is not just watching you, he is also telepathically tuning in to see if your thoughts are being formulated in the approved proper language. He can tell by the look on your face if you're thinking in French.

Martin represses English in our home more effectively than Irish has been suppressed by the English in Ireland. You might say that writing this novel in English is an act of retrospective resistance.

Nevertheless, if speaking English at home is considered by Martin the way other parents treat foul language in the mouths of their offspring, he acknowledges that it is the idiom of the country we reside in and that its influence cannot entirely be eradicated.

Since Hiberno-English must be tolerated as an inescapable evil, the contents, nature and geographical location of our English pronouncements are kept under tight surveillance. By geographical location I mean that Martin has apportioned our space in the house into linguistic zones, rather like a scaled down domestic version of post-war Berlin.

Cognizant of the fact that the local lingo is gaining ground in the house, he decides to tolerate home English only out in the front and back gardens and on the balcony where play is at its wildest and English is wont to burst out uncontrollably. Our backyard balcony is huge and the only one of its kind in Cork and Martin has had to acquire a special permit to build it.

When these geo-linguistic rules have been firmly established and for the most part strictly observed under threat of duress, Martin decides to lay down more linguistic legislation.

At breakfast one morning, he informs us that he never wants to hear the greeting word "Hi", even in the garden. It is an Americanism and for that reason alone cannot be tolerated. If we really must resort to English amongst ourselves in the vicinity of the house, he says, we are to have recourse to "Hello", a much healthier wholesome word. Its origin is far less reprehensible. Forewarned is forearmed. "Hi", we are told, is not to be uttered because it is American but also because it remains as a painful reminder of the German word "Heil." As well as this, anything remotely American is really to be shunned because, although we narrowly escaped being invaded by the Germans, we are willy-nilly unwittingly being colonized by American pop culture.

Legislation for the rules governing usage in French is much more severe and restrictive than this in the Montcocq household. Martin insists on teaching his children French as it was spoken in 1968, the year he left France, a few weeks after the student revolts broke out in Paris. He remarks that although the students caused an upheaval, they did not revolt against proper French.

Martin refuses entry to any new words that attempt to crop up over the next forty years. He decrees that there will be no more changes in the language. He sets up his own domestic branch of L'Académie Française which dictates proper usage, stigmatizes neologisms, frowns upon 1970s slang and actively hounds out any developing loan-words, especially if they are of Anglo-Saxon origin.

In our early years, as a consequence of these decrees, we are not permitted to pronounce "*un Walkman*" but are forced to call the device "*un baladeur.*" "*Un CD*", we are told, should at all times be replaced by the far more flowing collocation "*un disque compact.*" You shouldn't say "*un dealer*" but "*un revendeur de stupéfiants*" (a turn of phrase which no French person ever uses to my knowledge). Much later, in sadder times, after having suffered from too much tension at work, familial bickering and spousal coercion, he will tell us that we shouldn't say *"ton pacemaker"* but *"ton stimulateur cardiaque."*

In our youth, the strictures imposed on speech at the dinner table are so constraining that listening to one of the dining room radios in silence sometimes feels like a blessing in disguise. We often resort to communicating under the table by footsie if our father's long legs aren't blockading access.

In order to keep his and our mastery of French in good shape, the whole household is requested to listen to a multitude of programs on our father's favorite long-wave radio station. Martin keeps his wrist watch set at French time so he doesn't miss any bulletins or profoundly enlightening French chat shows, which means that he is generally an hour out of synch with Irish time, except for a few days when the seasonal timechange occurs at different set dates in each country.

For the whole duration of my childhood, we are subjected to massive doses of radio activity. When we get up in the morning, Martin's radio station is already blaring; the set is still on after our midday nap; it is still on when we go to bed in the evening. France Inter is broadcast to us all from strategic checkpoints in the house. There is a radio transmitter in the kitchen next to a painting of the Ascension of the Virgin, there is one in each bedroom, the dining room and the sitting room just above a reproduction of a hell scene by Bosch. Even the toilet is equipped with its own mini-radio, perched above the toilet between the toilet rolls on the shelf so that our father can listen to France Inter and gain additional knowledge about the world while moving his bowels.

I later discover that this is a traditional Francophone activity. The average Frenchman brings at least one magazine, an adult comic strip or a 600-page novel to the restroom; in his lavatory, our father listens to the radio in a state of liturgical silence, disposing of unwanted fecal matter.

Over the years, we thus endure, and almost learn to love, the domestic equivalent of Communist era crowd-gathering megaphones within our home, a secular version of the muezzin, calling us to prayerful reverence for the French language from tabletops and shelves. For years and years, we spend breakfast, lunch and dinner in boredom-burdened silence, for the most part pretending to pay attention to yet another particularly important moment in world news or French culture. Professor Montcocq is the strictest disciplinarian instructor we ever have to encounter. The iceberg-blue eyes of his rapt, speechless face as he listens intently are enough to reduce a berserker warrior to humility and silence.

Although later as an adult I refuse to let a single radio set anywhere near my apartment, I nevertheless emigrate to France. Three of my siblings become French teachers, my youngest brother becomes a UN interpreter, Sif gets severely addicted to internet newsreels in French, German, English and Chinese and Brian becomes a freelance bulletin reader for a number of networks.

You have just begun to witness the disciplinarian doppelgänger enthroned at the heart of Martin Montcocq. Born during the war years, but reaching full adulthood in the hippy age, Martin Montcocq's cerebral wiring is, as I have hinted, a somewhat complicated affair. In fact, as you will see, it is as convoluted and congested as the nest of electric wires on an Indian telegraph pole.

If you have seen *Terminator 3: Rise of the Machines*, you will understand what I mean. In the scene in which the robot played by Arnold Schwarzenegger has been outclassed, crushed and reprogrammed by a technologically superior terminator, he is given new orders to eliminate his former protégé John Connor. As this conflicts with his original programming, Arnold becomes so conflicted that he alternates between executing one order and its opposite command at the same time, leading to major malfunctioning.

Due to historical circumstances, Martin's values and priorities have undergone a similar resetting so that for the rest of his life he is left grappling with the contending forces of two behavioral codes, numerically encrypted in 1939 and 1968 respectively. Austerity, thrift, old-school discipline vs. baroque overspending and disorder. As a child of the Montcocq family, you are often allowed to experience these sets of character traits in alternation, or witness the spectacle of Martin Montcocq's brain experiencing both imperatives simultaneously.

As you will see in later chapters, Martin's sense of thrift will make him implement domestic austerity measures that would strain the credulity of a gull. But before his war-born thrift reflex kicks in, he is given to gradually more alarming bouts of hyper-generosity.

Martin is what one can only call an enthusiast. A generous soul who wishes humanity to prosper. When he reads an article about the merits of brushing teeth thrice a day, he buys toothbrushes for everyone he knows. If you come to the household, you are treated to a toothbrush within minutes of your entering. If he is invited for dinner, he brings toothbrushes instead of wine to the consternation of his hosts and the embarrassment of his wife and kids. Every single one of his 426 students that year is given a toothbrush.

Then one day for no apparent reason, the toothbrush fad fades and Martin takes a shine to flossing and soap, distributing the manna of floss kits and anti-septic soap bottles to all and sundry. When he begins to buy and gift bicycles by the dozen, our mother intervenes to remind him that his lecturer's salary will not take the strain.

Northern Ireland is brought under direct rule from Westminster. The first extraterrestrial message is sent from Earth into space. John Lennon is ordered to leave the United States in 60 days.

The World Trade Center opens in New York. Hammerin' Hank Aaron hits 715th HR, breaking Babe Ruth's record in Atlanta. The Pulitzer Prize is awarded to Robert Lowell.

The US performs nuclear tests at the Nevada Test Site. John Lennon reports seeing a UFO in New York. The US and East Germany establish diplomatic relations. Bob Dylan records "Blood on the Tracks." A race riot in Boston breaks out due to bussing. Christian Bale, James Blunt, Penelope Cruz, Hilary Swank, Joaquin Phoenix, Leonardo Di Caprio sign on. Georges Pompidou, Duke Ellington and Charles Lindbergh succumb.

5
Mrs. Cow's Crèche

The US Department of Interior proclaims the grizzly bear a threatened species. Ice thickness is measured at 4776 meters on Wilkes Land, Antarctica. Margaret Thatcher defeats Edward Heath for the leadership of the British Conservative Party. Portugal signs an accord for Angola's independence.

41 people are killed in the London Underground as a train rushes past the final stop. Dog spectacles are patented. Ethiopia ends its monarchy after 3000 years. Mick Jagger punches a restaurant window and is given 20 stitches.

My mother feels it is time I went to a day-care center. She is a bit irritable lately. This is more than understandable as my sisters and I are a bit of a pain in the neck, to put it politely. When she is preparing the meal, for instance, I scream that I am hungry until she is on the verge of banging my head with the frying pan. When the meal is finally ready, I refuse to eat and spit out the food that is forced into my mouth.

Why am I scolded for licking the toilet bowl? Another day I get a slap on the bottom for chewing a really interesting piece of black stuff I pull off the street with a stick, a wonderful piece of road that never gets smaller no matter how much you chew.

Mother doesn't like it when I try to push my head up her bottom, despite the fact that it gives me a very cozy feeling. The French doctor we go to see about it during the holidays says it's nothing to be worried about.

"He's trying to make contact with your uterus. If he continues to attempt it in his teens, consult me again."

I start hitting and prodding everyone in sight. I even poke Sif in the eye and Deirdre up the nostril. There's nothing like the feeling that I can topple Dad over on the bed as we wrestle. He says he would prefer just to hug but where's the fun in hugging? I want to knock, punch, pinch, poke.

The testosterone level in my body has suddenly doubled, but I only find that out 40 years later, browsing through an Empik bookshelf in Gdansk, Poland.

Anne has had enough of my behavior. She is pregnant again and tired and has Deirdre and Sif latched to each side of her or crawling under the table and the new baby Brian whimpering in his cot as she cooks. She decides I need to see a replacement mother for a while so she finds a family-run crèche. The lady in charge is literally called Mrs. Cow.

When I meet her in the flesh, I discover to my disappointment that there is nothing bovine about Mrs. Cow; on the contrary, she is a sweet, gentle woman with medium-sized breasts and curly ovine hair. Her husband, whom we rarely see, is a ruddy-complexioned man with thinning wisps of fox hair, a standard chest, a bit of a Guinness-induced pot belly and a no doubt average-sized penis which I thankfully never encounter.

Mrs. Cow's only defect, as far as I can see, is her sickly-looking son who is always watching us from the doorway as if to say "this is my mother and she is not yours: do not think that she loves you".

For some reason, he is generally gnawing away at a crust of Irish/British sandwich bread that's as white as his face. He leans against the doorframe and kneads a filthy-looking bit of bread dough in his fingers, staring at us vacantly, never batting an eyelid. We never say a word to each other and I remember him as little more than a blanched chewing mouth surrounded by a splattering of carrot-colored freckles and two large spaced-out eyes. I will never know how he turns out.

The days flick past in quick succession. I am at first disconcerted to be surrounded by so many unknown infants both smaller and larger. I play, play and play with cubes, fluffy toys, cowboys and Indians, crawl around on the thick-piled yellow carpet in search of bacteria. My mother is very fond of germs. She says they are so small you can't see them but they are there, everywhere, all over everything. This I need to check for myself. I want to tell her I've spotted a germ. I hunt for them everywhere and examine the tiniest recesses, but there are none to be found. She is evidently having me on about those creatures.

The other children have runny noses, and I exchange sloppy, open-mouthed kisses with any other infant who is willing. I still relish the flowing briny taste of good runny snot.

My stay at Mrs. Cow's crèche initiates twenty years of Irish colds, Irish pharyngitis, Irish tonsillitis, Irish hemorrhoids, Irish asthma, Irish flu, Irish eczema (behind the knees, on the shins, elbows, cleft of the bottom), Irish measles, Irish smallpox, Irish chickenpox and a mild form of pox of the Irish soul in later years.

When I see my father pissing in the sink one day, I stare in surprise. My father's French genitals are a complicated affair, a thick beige tube of wrinkle-skin swathed in a vast nest of hair. Although I am only 4 years old, he looks down towards me and says

"If you wish to feel French, micturate in the sink without letting your espoused one find out."

I ask him what an "espoused one" is and he says it's someone you have to live with for a long time. Irishmen, he continues, would never dare to micturate in the sink. They have been toilet-trained by their mothers and their wives and the British. The English are all "anal retentive", he adds. Although this is not easily verifiable and I haven't a clue what he's talking about, it seems like an important thing to remember.

The next day, we find and adopt a stray cat which my father names "Ayatollah." I'm not sure why, other than because he is always listening to people talking about that name on the radio. When I ask him, he says that Shah sounds like the French word for cat.

As you can see, talking to my father is a bit like reading *Alice in Wonderland*. I'm not sure I understand the logic of all the things he says, even 40 years later, but at the age of 4, I am already used to the fact that our father's mind works in mysterious ways. In any case Ayatollah is the name that sticks to the cat despite our efforts to name it according to the usual standards of feline nomenclature.

I now know how to spell my name and surname on the fridge in multi-colored magnet letters, and can dress from head to foot, tying even the buttons and laces, though sometimes I put the buttons in the wrong holes and squeal and grunt with irritation until the most nerve-wracked, exasperated parent helps me out.

I go around saying my name all day long, and sing Bah Bah Black Sheep, I Wish You a Merry Christmas, and the Wheels on the Bus Go Round and Round. I sing these for breakfast before we go to Mrs. Cow's place as loudly as I can at the table and then treat my parents to some more when they come and collect me. My mother teaches me other nursery rhymes so that they don't have to listen to the same songs to the point of torture. Old King Cole and Four and Twenty Blackbirds become the next hit singles at home, until they are replaced by Humpty Dumpty and This Little Piggy Went to Market; This Little Piggy Stayed Home.

The book illustrations for The Woman Who Lived in a Shoe hold my attention in a way that I don't quite understand. Little do I know at this point that the swarming multitude of children that afflicts the poor raddled woman is going to stream off the page into my own existence, over the next twenty years.

My life at this point is a finely-honed series of rituals and habits. On Saturdays, my father takes me to the park while mummy takes care of the twins and Brian and strokes and coos at the upcoming set of babies in the hump of her belly.

The moment we get there, my father whips a book out of his pocket while I roam around the park in search of interesting bits of fungus.

I have a passion for sticks. I wield them and bandy them and shout krrr! at every swipe as I hack through very bad people and wolves. Sticks as blood-soaked swords, sticks as unconscious polymorphously perverse penises, sticks as writing implements, sticks as mighty power symbols that jab and dissect. There is nothing I love more than to stir a puddle of mud or prod a dollop of frogspawn until the little spotted blobs of jelly come undone from each other.

My father places me at the top of the slide, goes back to reading his book, and expects me to plunge to my peril while he reads. I insist on being watched so he watches with a smile and a sigh, lowering his book for a few seconds. He prefers to push me on the swings so he can read without being interrupted, holding his book in one hand and pushing with the other. I say Higher! or Harder! and he pushes higher and harder, without realizing, so engrossed is he in his reading, that I am practically up in the clouds and on the verge of swinging the whole way around the bar. I make the most of this, developing a taste for the extreme.

On Sunday mornings, my father writes his Articles and my mother takes us to Church with the baby. At first this is fun as I am allowed to run around in the aisles with Deirdre and Sif, play dinkies with the boys, but lately our mother is trying to make us listen to what the priest is saying and that is an unbelievable bore, unless it's the story of Jonah and the whale - that's a funny one - and Moses opening up a dual carriageway in the Red Sea. I also like it when the Is Ray Lights get Manna during their Exit Us, although I can't understand why they don't bring more food along on a journey that long through the Wilderness. It strikes me as being unutterably careless. Even my father doesn't forget to bring a snack when he comes to fetch me from the day-care center.

The only part of the mass I enjoy is when we are asked by the priest to shake hands. I cherish the moment when the droning voice stops and anything seems possible. I shake and shake those neighborly hands. Anyone's hand is suddenly available for shaking. You're allowed to pull a grandmother's finger, if you feel like it.

When we get back from Church, we have to eat the meal that daddy has prepared, which is invariably boiled potatoes and broccoli and boiled fish with water sauce. Always a good girl, Deirdre swallows the bland, tasteless items down uncomplainingly, but Sif and I hate the food and have to be force-fed. The upshot is that we are later very easy to please. By the time we are fully trained, every child in the Montcocq family is both mentally and physically equipped to eat anything and find it tasty. You could sling a rock on our plates, we would eat it. Dump a dollop of earth in our bowls with the porridge, we would consume it and be ready to discuss the merits of minerals.

On Sunday afternoons, my father takes me and the twins out to the woods to collect kindle for the fire while he saws fallen branches into logs we can dump into the back of the car and drive home. He shows us how to hold a saw and thrust it into the branch. It slices and releases the wood smell. The sawdust hangs over the branch in sun-dancing particles. My father is proud that I can lift the heaviest logs and manage to place them in an orderly way in the boot. He sings our praises to mummy and Brian the toddler when we get back.

My father has a prickly cactus of a face, but he's a nice daddy nonetheless. He holds my hand in the evenings after mother has read stories to us from the Old Testament. When he is about to get up, I ask him to hold both of my hands in one of his and both of my feet in the other. Sif and Deirdre want the same. He does it to all of us and chuckles and then plugs in the tape-recorder and plays Beethoven's Fifth Symphony every night. We say Leave the door open and then leave the music on and we add Promise, he says I promise, Promise, I promise, Promise ok. He says I love you too, we say we love you three, we love you four, and so on up to twenty.

As he walks out of the room, we play kiss tennis: we blow him a kiss and he smack-blows it back. We play sets that last so long most of us fall asleep before the end of the match.

Mummy goes into hospital one day and we bring her flowers, chocolates and oranges. This time she brings home two small babies. Una and Aidan. I now count two brothers and three sisters.

When I try to tickle Una, she cries. My father calls Brian, Deirdre and Sif 'toddlers' and it's true they do toddle a lot. Brian calls me Ulf on the good days, and Uh-Uh-Uh when he gets excited. Deirdre and Sif have an annoying habit of trying to snatch my willy in the bathtub to see how far they can stretch it.

One day, our parents invent a new family concept which anticipates the American notion of quality time. My father calls it the *excellente soirée*. It means getting together in the sitting room about once a week. We all sit on the sofa, the different-sized toddlers propped up with cushions so that they look as if they are sitting of their own accord like little grown-ups. The record player is put on with Jacques Brel, Edith Piaf, Julos Beaucarne, Gilles Vigneault or classical music, and we listen and look at each other and the fire. We say what a lovely evening it is.

Then the music is lowered and we talk for a while and have cakes and juice, or tea and oranges to the sound of Leonard Cohen. For the time being, Leonard is still enjoying life with Jane and Suzanne so it's just mellow and soothing and not all that gloomy.

The Excellente Soirée is concluded by a token of communal love which is left over from our father's hippy days. To begin with, the activity is called *La Bise à 6*, but it has now expanded to *La Bise à 8* to include Una and Aidan. Translated, the phrase describes group-kissing on the mouth.

In a closely-knit circular queue, we all stand with babies and toddlers held aloft so our faces are at the same level. The idea is to bestow our mouths on everyone more or less simultaneously. In theory, if nobody pushes his or her face in too pressingly this should mean that you only get a corner of the family lips, no matter how much you pucker and project your mouth, but in practice Martin's kisses are voracious and sloppy and you come out feeling that half of your face has been mouthed by a prickly army of snails.

Some of my siblings are less reticent than I am, engaging in saliva-stringing abandon, giving rise to unusual forms of filial piety and sibling competition. Imagine an innocently incestuous kissing-orgy fueled by mutual affection and zest and you will have an idea of collective queue-kissing in the household.

Outside our house, my (only partially true) impression is that Irish family law has prohibited touching between fathers and sons. Contact is allowed when a hard slap on the back is required to indicate approval and in cases where a boot must be applied to a buttock as a sign of reproof. These are the official recommendations, but it is a little-known fact that a number of Irish families fail to observe them.

Cars in the Netherlands adopt seatbelts. The trial against the Baader-Meinhof group begins in Stuttgart. Muhammad Ali defeats Joe Bugner in Malaysia. Hank Williams Jr. survives a suicidal fall off the side of Ajax Peak in Montana. Dmitri Shotakovitch is buried. Viking 1 is launched to orbit around Mars. Communists take over Laos. The first Assassination attempt on US President Gerald Ford is carried out in Sacramento. Rembrandt's *Nightwatch* is slashed.

Papua New Guinea gains independence from Australia. Soviet spacecraft Venera 9 soft-lands on Venus, caressing its mons. The Netherlands grants Suriname independence. Drew Barrymore, Angelina Jolie, Charlize Theron, Moon Bloodgood, Kate Winslet, Mila Jovovich and Tiger Woods begin their lives. P.G. Wodehouse, Chiang Kai-shek, Josephine Baker, Eamon de Valera, Francisco Franco and Pier Paolo Pasolini come to an end.

6
Skin and Bones and Hair

The first commercial Concorde flight takes off. The United States vetoes a United Nations resolution that calls for an independent Palestinian state. Twelve bombs explode in the West End of London. In Guatemala and Honduras an earthquake kills more than 22,000. As a measure to curb population growth, the minimum age for marriage in India is raised to 21 years for men and 18 years for women. The UK and Iceland end the Cod War. The Soweto uprising in South Africa begins.

Our father brings home two of his international students. They are going to stay with us as lodgers. We feel immensely honored that the only two Black Men in the city of Cork are to be lodged in our house. It is a totally mesmerizing experience as in 1976 there are no Africans to speak of in Ireland.

They stand before us at the door. We stare and stare at Joseph and Simon and Simon smiles back, all ebony glow and luminescent ivory. At the table, in front of them, the twins ask my mother why Joseph and Simon are brown. She is embarrassed but Simon laughs good-heartedly and says they are both from Nigeria.

Later, when they are in their rooms, Deirdre asks mummy again and she tells us they are dark because the sun is so strong in Africa. They are protecting themselves from the sun. Joseph is an Igbo from Biafra and Simon is from the north of Nigeria.

Although they talk to each other regularly in a language that we do not understand, very soon you can feel a palpable tension between the two lodgers.

Simon is as sweet as it's possible to be. He even lets the four twins and I touch his huge nest of hair. Sif focuses all her attention on kneading his ears. Simon's hair is an endless source of pleasure. To us, Simon is the King of Nigeria crowned with a bubble bath nest of bunchy-bobbing black hair. Honeycomb hive hair, licorice-colored candy floss, full of spring-foam and moss, a frizz of a hairbloom. We spend hours playing with it, pulling it, molding it, examining it, dry-shampooing the thick sprawling growth into all kinds of topiary. Only much later when I knead the firm elastic breasts of my first teenage girlfriend will I feel such elastic ecstasy in handling.

Simon seems to like it most of the time, though sometimes he is sick of it. But now he is laughing with a pleased and only slightly embarrassed chuckle. Mother says that's enough! We are to leave Simon in peace.

Joseph is different. His hair is much shorter and we are disinclined to touch it. He doesn't invite us to and his gaze is enough to put you off considering the idea. He doesn't laugh freely or as often as Simon, and when he does it is a hard, mirthless cough that shatters on the ear. He doesn't look at us much and generally keeps to himself during meals, concentrating on his food, speaking briefly only when he is asked a direct question and even then reluctant to engage in any form of conversation.

Joseph leaves his plate impeccably, immaculately clean and is able to do something which greatly impresses my siblings and me. When we have chicken or pork chops or beef on the bone, he takes the bones in his hands and snaps them in front of us. He is able to put bone pieces into his mouth and suck thin worms of marrow clean out of their sockets. We can hardly believe that bones can be snapped and that they have extra-good nourishment stored secretly inside. Our mother says that marrow is very nutritious. It is really the best part of the meat. We want marrow too but our teeth and our lips are incapable of extracting it.

As the weeks pass, tension starts building between Simon and Joseph, and then between Joseph and my parents. Joseph has stopped paying the rent. At first, he claims that the money will be arriving shortly, but in the end it doesn't arrive at all.

One day my mother asks him for the rent during dinner. His answer leaves an uncomfortable, cemetery silence at the table.

"I have decided not to pay for the room."

"Excuse me?"

"I have decided not to pay the rent that you are asking. It is too high, and the children are too noisy. They run around all the time and I have to queue in front of the toilet and the bathroom. I sometimes wait twenty minutes to have breakfast. As well as this, it is cold in your house. I have to keep a blanket around my shoulders when I am studying to stop shivering."

"Cold? Joseph, this is Ireland."

"Jesus, Joseph," our father adds, "why do you not switch on the heating device installed in your room?"

"The heater is on, but the room remains cold. It is humid."

"As you say, Ireland is a cold, humid country," my mother exclaims, "but that doesn't make accommodation free!"

"I will not pay for the room."

Looking extremely tense and threatening now, Joseph takes a bone off his plate, extends his hand slowly, points the bone at the two gurgling twins like a kapo in a concentration camp and snaps it between his fingers. He drops the two bits of bone in the middle of the table like a gauntlet.

Simon is breathing deeply, looking mortified and scared.

Joseph picks up another bone from his plate. Looking at my parents in silence, he begins to press the tip of the bone into his own cheekbone, just below the eye, harder and harder until finally his hand trembles and the bone breaks. The top half of the bone drops into his plate.

A pearl of blood appears below Joseph's cheekbone where the lower half of the bone has stabbed him. As if he hasn't noticed, Joseph chucks the bloody end of the half-bone into his mouth like someone throwing a match into a fireplace. He closes his mouth and begins to suck out the marrow, the tip of the bone sticking out of his lips.

He looks me in the eye with a gaze I am unable to define, a stare that makes me want to stay still and lower my eyes to my plate. He looks round the table at every one of us and crunches the piece of bone between his teeth.

Our parents look as if they have just seen a cluster of tarantulas crawl up out of the sink. Simon is sitting as straight as a tree. He whispers something peevishly to Joseph. A few minutes later, without saying a word, Joseph gets up calmly and goes to his room.

When Joseph is safely out of earshot, Simon tells our father that Joseph's parents both died of starvation during the Nigerian civil war.

"You know, his village had to resort to –"

"To?"

"Well, you know what can happen in times of acute famine. It happened also in Ukraine when Stalin starved the population to death. When the Nigerian forces of my country blockaded Biafra, two million people died of starvation and war. Terrible things happened."

"We're sorry to hear what happened to your country, but terrible as it is, it doesn't justify not paying the rent."

"Joseph is not a bad man," he adds, "he is just totally traumatized."

From then onwards, our parents take to locking the door of our bedrooms. At first, they do it discreetly, barely daring to turn the key in case Joseph overhears them, but then one evening my father decides to do it ostentatiously making a loud key-scraping noise and turning the key with an off-putting snap.

Joseph begins to smoke in the kitchen and the sitting room and when my father asks him to take his cigarette out to the patio, Joseph takes to smoking in his room. Our parents are afraid of a fire hazard, so they begin to leave our rooms unlocked again and spend the nights in fear of the creaking of floorboards, the brushing of wind against windows.

And then one day, Joseph is gone. He leaves without a word or a check or a note. He takes the key along with him and the door is left locked. When our father breaks the door with a crowbar, we discover a thick smell of smoke. There are cigarette burns on the sheets and the ash-freckled mattress. One of the burn holes is so deep I can stick my entire forefinger through the sheet, deep into the guts of the mattress.

The Pleasures of Queueing

Joseph disappears and Martin Montcocq never catches sight of him again at University. Simon says he thinks he has gone to Limerick.

My mother performs *damnatio memoriae* on the room, throwing out sheets, blankets and mattress, but Joseph and what happened to his family lingers in our minds for a long time.

Simon stays on in the house and offers to babysit for my parents to atone for his compatriot's behavior. He teaches us songs from his homeland. We learn the lyrics in Yoruba, whole verses off by heart without knowing what it means. The sounds that come out of Simon's mouth are more than beautiful and they make his eyes glitter. He is invariably soft-spoken and gentle and lets us dip our hands into his hair when our parents aren't looking. Sif has gone back to massaging his earlobes.

He sits there, the picture of patience, a little embarrassed but smiling and sometimes I think he likes it and sometimes he looks a bit sad and we don't know what he's thinking. I never meet a kinder, sweeter man.

*

After wiping his mouth with the floor-cloth after dinner, our Franco-Italian great-grandfather dies in Nice of a heatstroke at the age of 97, having continued to repair shoes in his shoemaker's shop until the day before his death. He has always put the shit-blotched, pavement-worn, tubercular-spit-stained soles of his customers' shoes straight into his mouth as he hammers at the leather thus ensuring his perfect immunity to everything under the sun including Ebola and Typhoid.

When they strip his body for embalming, the morticians discover that our great-grandfather was both shower and bath-shy, though we distinctly remember him claiming that he took a bath every Christmas whether he needed it or not. His fishnet tank-top has literally grown into the skin on his back. One of the embalmers says it is so worn out and embedded in the dermis that our ancestor must have kept it on for decades.

Martin Montcocq's thrift and fearless attitude to bacteria is finally discovered to be hereditary.

Behind the fireplace, our grandmother finds an embarrassment of gold that her father has hidden away in a box while continuing to eat nothing but soup, bread and chocolate for breakfast, lunch and dinner.

We call our great-grandfather Pépé Bonboni because he always has sweets in one of his pockets. We are encouraged to burrow inside his clothes to find the lucky pocket. When the embalmers give us his clothes, Martin finds five sweets in his coat.

Pépé Bonboni is now a box full of ash, wood, skin and bone. When our grandmother isn't looking, we take the urn down from the mantelpiece, screw the top off and push fingers into the debris. The flakes stick to our hands and lodge under the nails.

Our mother's belly is bigger and rounder than ever. She wobbles around, always on the point of tottering. With her elasticated pants drawn up over her bellybutton, she looks like a tender, soft-boiled human egg perched on an eggcup.

Strikes start in Poland after the communists raise food prices. Palestinian extremists hijack an Air France airplane. Seychelles gains independence from the United Kingdom. In New York City, the Son of Sam pulls a gun from a paper bag, killing one and seriously wounding another, in the first of a series of attacks that terrorize the city for a year. The chimpanzee is placed on the list of endangered species.

NASA releases the famous Face on Mars photo, taken by Viking 1. Ten thousand Protestant and Catholic women demonstrate for peace in Northern Ireland. The first known outbreak of Ebola virus occurs in Yambuku, Zaire. The Irish rock band U2 is formed after drummer Larry Mullen posts a note looking for members for a band on the notice board of his Dublin school.

Clarence Norris, the last known survivor of the Scottsboro Boys, is pardoned. The first megamouth shark is discovered off Oahu in Hawaii. At least 3,840 are killed in a Richter scale magnitude 7.3 earthquake in Turkey. Colin Farrell and Soleil Moon Frye check in. Agatha Christie, Howard Hughes and Mao Zedong discontinue their lives.

7
Ireland and Hemorrhoids

Leonard Cohen releases his new record, *Death of a Ladies' Man*. Snow falls in Miami for the only time in its history. The Massacre of Atocha takes place during the Spanish transition to democracy. London's *International Times* declares that punk is dead. The first issue of the science fiction comic strip *2000 AD* is launched. *Star Wars* opens in cinemas. The rings of Uranus are discovered.

When I get back to school after the summer holidays, a chart has been put up at the back of the classroom. It's a grid, one of those charts designed to make you feel you're the dumbest creature that ever walked the Earth.

I've missed the teacher's explanations because of compulsive day-dreaming, a dysfunctional lack of concentration which I later discover is really undiagnosed Attention Deficit Disorder. I haven't a clue what to do with the chart. Someone explains to me at the break that we are supposed to look up at the sky, assess the general shape of the clouds and write down the right answer in the corresponding box. That much I knew.

A cloudless sky in Ireland is a virtually unheard-of phenomenon, which unfortunately means that there is a great variety of cloud shapes to identify.

When one day it comes around to my turn, our teacher, having gathered that Olaf lost and lowly is slow to cop on, appoints the best boy in the class to teach me during the break how the grid works and what I'm supposed to put in it.

The best boy enlightens me about Cirriform, Stratocumuliform and Stratiform, words I find totally incomprehensible. There is also Cirrus Fibrates, he adds, and Cirrus Unicus, Cirrus Spissatus, Cirrus Castellanus, Cirrus Floccus, Cirrus Fibratus Invertebratus.

By the time the best boy with superhuman powers of concentration gets to the next subspecies of cloud, I have stopped listening and am just thinking about how the hell I am going to remember any of this and find the Right Answer on any given day.

The brainy boy leaves and I am left on my own in the class with an open felt-tip marker in my hand. Brainy boy is also a lick and has refused to give me the Right Answer. I go to the window to look at the clouds. Just thick cotton as far as the eye can see. It's a lie that every cloud has a silver lining. The ones in Ireland are all grey on the sides and white in the middle.

Occasionally, when the sun is able to stuff a ray between clouds, the light is granted a few seconds of glory to shine straight onto Ireland and you catch a glimpse of your shadow. You are able to witness the unsuspected presence of your twin materialize in front of you. The darkness of your shadow self gives you a sense of real weight and matter, but it quickly disappears. The sun retreats behind cloud and you are left weightless and alone.

My aunt has told me that the skies are covered with puff pastries laid out every morning by Saint Patrick, but that piece of knowledge isn't much use to me now. I realize suddenly that the morning break is about to end and I still don't know what to write on the chart. I wave in desperation to someone outside the window, point to the sky with my marker and lift my shoulders with an air of catastrophe. The kid outside lifts his eyes momentarily to the sky, raises his hands on each side to mean "don't ask me, boy, I'm as thick as you are", and runs off.

My asthma starts to rev its engine up and I feel cloud formations enter my lungs. Some of the kids are starting to make noise at the other end of the corridor. They're all about to come back, and the teacher right after them. I'll be the laughing stock of the school.

I don't know what to write, I don't even know how to spell the different types of clouds. I put the tip of the marker on the rectangle in the chart, quickly scribble Serious Fluckus just in time to scramble back to my seat.

Miraculously, the teacher says this is the Right Answer and even compliments me, but I still get a jeer from Leila and Caroline because the spelling is wrong. Spelling is not my forte and it takes another decade for me to have a shaky mastery over this inhumane invention.

We have also started learning Irish, but my ADD makes sure that I quickly fall behind most of the others in my class. They seem to understand what the teacher is saying when she starts to speak Gaelic as if the language is already in their veins. But it's all Greek to me. Double Dutch Gobbledygook. I haven't a clue what she is saying. Not an iota. I feel myself barely able to stay afloat in a vast sea of sounds, and this feeling of helpless meaninglessness returns whenever we do Irish.

Much later, in secondary school, I discover that most of my fellow-pupils are actually as ignorant as I am and couldn't be bothered with Irish. The level of motivation is low. The British are gone, leaving their language behind them. It's ours now and Irish is little more than an alien tongue that teachers try to graft into our mouths, trying to colonize our brains with useless dead words, stuffing the whole Irish flag down our throats, expecting us to speak.

Gaelic words slip off our tongues like water off a duck. For most of us, the language is primeval muck, the kind of mud that you'd like to wipe off your shoes but it's out of the question until you leave school. We are to keep walking through the goo until we reach the outskirts of the bog.

When I get to the Leaving Certificate oral at the age of eighteen, I still don't know what most of the words mean. The examiner is a joyfully smiling little man with hale ruddy cheeks, sweet as a leprechaun, the kind of little cobbler you see illustrated in books, cobbling away at the language of his heart in his backwater, reed-woven cottage. I like him instantly and feel sorry that I have so little Gaelic to offer. When he hears me stumble through my back-broken Irish, it will be like throwing a bucket of cold water into the hearth of his heart.

He asks me to read a poem on the course so I read. This I can do rather well as I've been hearing the language for a decade and play several musical instruments. Not understanding a word of the poem, I recite it like a swan song, pouring feeling by the bucket-load into every clause, playing the poem like a fiddle.

When I lift my eyes from the page, the leprechaun is glowing. His eyes are ablaze, his chest is a bellows. I feel so much pity for what is to come next, I try to hold his smile for as long as it will last. When he asks me a question and then another and another, his face starts to sink into sadness and resentment.

Meanwhile, back in 1977, it begins to rain again and Mrs Sweetham switches back to comprehensible English sounds, telling us about Oisin and how he stole the Salmon of Knowledge.

It rains on my childhood and into my ears. Little do I suspect as I wade through the mud and the rain that less than twenty years later, I will be able to flee Irish weather, becoming the first climatic refugee in the family.

One day in spring, my home-grown hemorrhoids become so itchy my mother is forced to consult our local doctor. The GP is a thick-set man with a massive skull. He sits monumentally behind his desk and does not look at me a single time during the consultation.

"How long have you had piles?"

"I'm sorry?"

"How long has your son had piles?"

"Piles of what? You mean hemorrhoids. He's been itching for a year."

"Hmm. Internal or external?"

"External only, I think. Do you have them inside too, pet?"

I nod, not knowing what to say.

"Here's a prescription for corticosteroid cream. Is there anything else the matter with the boy?"

Now compare this to when my father makes me consult a French doctor during the summer holidays when my hemorrhoids stage a vengeful comeback, inside and outside.

Here's a word-for-word translation of the consultation:

"Take your clothes off and get up on the table, on your knees. That's it, now bend over with your head touching the table."

After that, I'm given to experience the comforts provided by a latex-gloved, petroleum-jellied hand rummaging around in my rear. To my wide-eyed dismay, this body cavity search goes on for what feels like at least twenty minutes.

The doctor is stretching my sphincter and colon way past their elastic limits. He even starts humming a tune as if he has forgotten what he is looking for, daydreaming about God knows what in the circumstances. Cheerfully, he ferrets and forages his way up my gut, giving me the distinct feeling he thinks he is fumbling around for car keys in his wife's recalcitrant handbag.

My mother is looking out the window.

I finally get back down off the table feeling I've been scoured with an overlarge bottle brush.

"There's a little inflammation in the lower rectum. Nothing very serious, but we may need to look into it. You can have it removed surgically. You can also have it stapled or he can be given an internal plaster that will inhibit further swelling. Or I can prescribe corticosteroid cream. Which would you prefer? I would recommend the ointment for the external hemorrhoids and leave the internal one alone for the time being. Tell me, has he been experiencing stress in any form, possibly at school?"

"Well, he's just started Irish and he's still having trouble with learning the names of the clouds."

"I see. Well, if it doesn't get better, I would advise you to make another appointment for the same time next month. And make sure he keeps taking that inhaler."

This is not to say that Irish doctors are mediocre, but in 1977 they have yet to acquire a more hands-on approach, which is, you might argue, lucky for the resilience of my sphincter.

Later in the year, my asthma attacks get so intense I have to spend three weeks in hospital for special preventive treatment. Asthmatic readers (that's one in ten of us) will know what asthma feels like.

Just in case you haven't enjoyed asthma yet, here's a description of what it's like so that you'll be able to interpret the symptoms when it hits you - it'll be one in three soon enough if all goes well in the merry world of industry.

When an asthma attack is on its way, you begin to feel that your chest is tight as a drum, itchy as a nettle. Then your palate starts needing a tongue rub. Then you feel a whistling sensation in your lungs and shortly afterwards, before you know it, it feels like you've inadvertently breathed in a hiveful of wasps who are themselves wondering where the queen wasp has got to and why it's all so dark of a sudden.

Then you cough out a wasp or two along with a few wet flakes of hive paper and you wait for the other frantic wasps buzzing in your lungs to die a slow, painful death, preferably before you do.

After about an hour or two, most of the insects in your chest have bitten the dust and you can subside into enjoying the soothing comforts of Darth Vader breathing.

In the hospital, they give me injections, pills to swallow, inhalers of various shapes and sizes to inhale. I am in a respiratory disease unit for small children whose lungs have failed to thrive on fossil-fuel emissions and the wonders of humidity-sodden, acarid-infested, wall-to-wall carpeting.

At night, I and the other asthma-sufferers get up and run around wheezing, whizzing through the corridors in search of adventure. One night, we even get our hands on a whole set of syringes. If you have ever tried this, you will know that a syringe is probably the best children's toy ever invented. It's safer when you take out the needle, of course. Filled with tap water, a massive syringe becomes a multi-purpose weapon. You wander round the hospital corridors feeling like the Six Million Dollar Man with bionic implants that make you move in slow-motion with a silent mental ticking sound.

Scientists report using bacteria in a lab to make insulin via gene splicing. *Never Mind the Bollocks* is released in the United Kingdom. Despite the fact that my teacher has told me that matter cannot be destroyed, Maria Callas and Charley Chaplin begin to dematerialize. Groucho Marx dies of pneumonia. Elvis Presley dies of fast food. Orlando Bloom, Shakira, Jessica Chastain, Victoria Crown Princess of Sweden, Tom Hardy and Maggie Gyllenhaal start to grow.

8
The Expectant Bishop

The European Court of Human Rights finds the British government guilty of mistreating prisoners in Northern Ireland. Richard Chase, the 'Vampire of Sacramento', is arrested. The People's Republic of China daringly lifts a ban on works by Aristotle, William Shakespeare and Charles Dickens. The next day, Little Nell is rearing to fight on the barricades of Tienanmen Square. Charlie Chaplin's remains are stolen from Corsier-sur-Vevey in Switzerland. Rhodesia attacks Zambia. Dick Smith tows a fake iceberg into Sydney Harbor.

Jimmy Carter decides to delay the production of the neutron bomb, a weapon which kills people with radiation but leaves buildings almost intact. The One Love Peace Concert is held at National Heroes Stadium in Kingston. Bob Marley unites two opposing political leaders at this concert, bringing peace to the war-ridden streets of the city. Charon, a satellite of Pluto, is discovered. A bombing by Breton nationalists causes destruction in the Palace of Versailles. John Paul II becomes pope. Abortion is legalized in Italy.

It is now time for my Holy Communion and the absorption of the sacraments. I have been subjected to hours and hours of Catholic catechism so I know that the renewable body of Christ is literally, bodily contained in the host.

My expectations for this event are high and I can hardly wait to find out what a slice of Christ will do on the tongue. I have been closely observing people's expressions when they receive the host. Nobody bothers to look at the face of the faithful when they open their mouths and stick out their tongues to incorporate the Body of Christ. Some members of the congregation look as if the host is being deposited on a particularly sensitive erogenous zone. Others look like my father when he is listening to Jacques Brel after a long day at work. Touched on the sanctified tongue by the holy wafer, some believers queueing for the host look like they have just been given a potent dose of cyanide and expect to die within minutes.

They all believe that this is the Body of Christ and that particular reverence and gravitas is required in the chewing.

I am so eager to experience the host, I'm almost wetting my pants.

When at last it is time for me to pronounce my vows for Communion, the priest holds the host in the air, ready to place the white coin of the Eucharist on my outstretched organ of taste. The buds on my tongue are fizzing, practically popping off my mouth. When the priest lowers his hand towards my saliva, I'm so gung-ho I could bite his fingers. And then before I know it, the host is on my tongue and I have Christ in my mouth.

Although Christ tastes exactly the same as the wafer my mother puts in our ice-creams, the moment is nevertheless intense. And yet, I am somewhat disconcerted that there is no really observable ecstasy in my body or my soul. Is this because my host is malfunctioning? Is my soul out of order? Has some glitch in the transubstantiation process made the host I got defective?

I also discover that the host is adhesive and hard to prize off the palate. I have to spend the rest of the mass trying to scrape the graft off with my tongue and my finger and when I manage to chew it (despite the fact that Deirdre says chewing it is a sin), the paste gets stuck in my teeth.

The experience is ultimately a little disappointing but still very far from the heartbreaking sense of existential absurdity I'm afflicted with when I get older.

The priest says mass and asks for a *silent* collection. I know from experience that *silent* does not mean we are to do it without noise. It's a euphemistic clerical code word for "no coins, please, only banknotes in the platter."

As we leave the Church of the Real Pleasure, we dip our fingers in the font. Only ten years later when I lose my virginity to a French Erasmus Student, do I feel as grand and manly as now.

Outside, it is raining as usual. My mother and my grandmother are radiant under their umbrellas. They are happy beyond bliss and keep showering compliments on my graphite-grey suit and lovely-blue tie. Thanks to the rain, I now feel knotted and ensconced in a wet textile envelope.

On the sloping esplanade in front of the church, my father takes about 500 photos. A number of our parents' friends give me presents and envelopes padded with £10 Jonathan Swift banknotes. Three people stuff balled up bills into my hand, forcing my fingers into a fist over the money and holding them pressed tightly together so that I don't look at the ball in my hand. This is Irish modesty and discretion at its best. Oh, the silent confection of origami bank balls!

From then onwards, my mother makes me go to Confession once a week. Unbeknownst to us at the time, the Pope has asked head priests in Ireland not to denounce their pedophile colleagues, so going to Confession is actually like playing Russian roulette without realizing you are playing.

Confession at the church I go to takes place not in a Confession booth but a room where you have to face the priest and tell him all your most intimate secrets. The problem is that I have little to tell. At this stage in my life I don't really have any secrets worth telling. The discovery of masturbation hasn't occurred to me yet so I can't show contrition for molesting myself. I cannot yet confess to the wicked wiles of wanking. The closest I come to wondering about the secondary attributes of my urine dispenser is thinking that Willy Wonka is a curiously embarrassing name.

Sexual fantasies are years away too. The only gratifying mental images my brain can conceive of at this point do not go beyond exchanging hellos with a girl down the block and holding her gaze for more than two seconds.

Confession is a vastly boring part of my Sunday afternoons for the next seven years until it dawns on me that I can skip it and no one will know. Sometimes I am so bored I would welcome the prospect of a pedophile priest to rebuff or accommodate.

But I am lucky at Irish roulette. Never once in seven years do I have to deal with priestly penetration, pontifical penis, sanctified sodomy, Brotherly blowjobs or Fatherly fingering. The closest I ever come to boredom-alleviating abuse is the odd priest's eager interest in my secrets, a lusty stare at my thick, rose-red lips, but nothing remotely resembling priestly petting.

The poor men deserve credit for that, considering the fact that there are no Gay and Lesbian clubs to join in 1970s Ireland, and no libido-dampening pills are dispensed to the clergy the way they are in the navy.

I am not making light of the traumatizing excesses that are perpetrated in the name of Christianity, only giving credit to the clergy where credit is due. I think of those poor prostrate priests lying in their beds at night, having to hold back increasingly overwhelming libidos, the reptilian brain deep at the center of their cortexes egging them on to disperse as much seed as they can.

The original idea the Catholic Church is trying to get at is the conservation of libidinal energy for the worship of God. And it does work, to some extent. If you consider the glow in the eyes of any given member of the priesthood in conversation with a particularly appealing member of the congregation, and then look at most members of the secular population talking to each other, you notice that the only human beings who look in any way erotically alive are your poor haggard priests. As someone once put it, sex is like air: it's no big deal, unless you're not getting any.

The problem with the idea behind priestly abstention is that sublimation doesn't work all that well. Your average priest looks at your average Bible with about as much joy and devotion as you or I might feel in the contemplation of a blackboard left blank.

One might ask why the stereotype of the priest is a big-bellied Father. Well, to begin with, there's the essential comfort-eating made necessary by the withering emotional deprivation of not being able to snuggle into your partner's arms or wriggle your worm into a wet willing vagina.

There's also the fact that the massive absorption of Guinness and Murphy imbibed to put the penis and the emotional deficit to sleep inevitably expands the intestinal cavity.

But despite the obesity of some members of the clergy, priests in Ireland are revered as demi-gods in 1978. Nearly a 100% of the population goes to Church at least once a week, divorce is still considered a religious crime and abortion is not a word you pronounce in polite company, or in any company really. People who have been standing in a queue for an hour will spread like courtiers before royalty when a Father honors the footpath with the soles of his socked, sandaled feet. Any self-respecting soul enjoying public transport will cross itself when the bus passes within even distant view of a church. Even if the church is set apart a mile away from the route as the bus passes, a flurry of hands will still flitter up.

Nobody knows at this point that out of the public eye the Most Reverend Roman Catholic Bishop Casey has been privately enjoying the sins of the flesh and is hiding a three-year-old son.

The Republic of Ireland's second television channel RTÉ 2 is broadcast for the first time. Ethiopia begins a massive offensive in Eritrea. Louise Brown, the world's first test-tube baby, is born in Manchester. Menachem Begin and Anwar Sadat begin the peace process at Camp David. Vietnam attacks Cambodia. Jimmy Carter signs a bill into law which allows for the home-brewing of beer in America.

Californian voters defeat the Briggs Initiative, prohibiting gay school teachers. The Soviet Union nuclear weapons stockpile exceeds the United States nuclear weapons stockpile. James Franco, Zoe Saldana, and Rachel McAdams grace the world with their presence. Pope Paul IV and Pope John Paul I pop their clogs in quick succession.

9

Cheese and Choice

Vietnam-backed Cambodian insurgents announce the fall of Phnom Penh and the collapse of the Pol Pot regime. Former Sex Pistols bassist Sid Vicious dies of a heroin overdose in New York. Ayatollah Khomeini comes to power in Iran. The People's Republic of China invades northern Vietnam.

The US Voyager I space probe photographs reveal Jupiter's rings. President Jimmy Carter is attacked by a swamp rabbit while fishing in his hometown in Georgia. A Soviet bio-warfare laboratory at Sverdlovsk accidentally releases airborne anthrax spores, killing 66 people and many innocent cows.

100 Schoolchildren in the Central African Republic are killed for protesting against compulsory school uniforms. Sweden outlaws corporal punishment in the home. The One Child Policy is introduced in parts of China, preventing about 400 million births.

Despite widespread neo-Malthusian fears that the massive increase in the world population is going to cause starvation, widespread war and pandemics in the near future, our parents persist in having over a baby a year.

As our mother insists on breast-feeding each of her children until the age of six, a quarrelsome extra queue starts to form in front of Anne Montcocq's breasts, several times a day. Inevitably, there is jostling and prodding, groping, grabbing and haggling over who should gain access to the most lactiferous bosom. Anne settles these contentions with amused Marian detachment.

Over the years, in times when over-crowding in the house becomes particularly intolerable, the elders (Deirdre, Sif, Brian and me) convene to discuss possible solutions to our parents' disastrous nativity rate. In hushed tones, the four of us plot to tie Anne's tubes in a knot, to nip Martin's testicles straight in the bud.

The first time we assemble, we agree to make our point discreetly by placing a packet of extra-resistant condoms on our father's bedside table. But the packet of contraceptives reappears in the middle of the breakfast table the next morning and we find ourselves browbeaten into religious contemplation of God's bountiful fluids.

The next time the committee convenes, we opt for more stringent measures. Deirdre proposes to set in motion what she calls *coitus interruptus*. The idea is to kick up a fuss or start a screaming match just outside our parents' door while they're actively engaged in making babies. Other tactics include pretending that one of the little ones is choking, or barging into the room accidentally on purpose, the moment their groaning and moaning starts to crescendo. We get the little ones to carry out Operation Interruptus so that it will look unplanned and spontaneous.

These policies have some effect, but they only delay conception by a month or two at best each time we try them, so the governing body of our committee votes to introduce even tougher measures. Brian offers to sprinkle pesticide on all of Martin's five underpants. When that doesn't work, he peppers them with rat poison.

We put pesticide and rat poison and toxic detergent in our father's eau-de-cologne, our mother's perfume, but all our attempts at dampening our parents' fertility is fruitless. The resistance of Martin's French testicles is a force to contend with and Anne continues to be visited by Angel Gabriel every single year.

After long years of failure, we are forced to concede that we will have to wait patiently for the menopause.

There are now nine of us, which means that I have to share my Lego pieces with the other elders. My building blocks have already been appropriated and dispersed to the four corners of the house and the garden by the little ones.

Deirdre and Sif take a lively interest in my Action Men, despite the fact that they have their own Cindies and Barbies. I don't mind this too much as long as they follow my ideas on how an Action Man should behave. If they help me catch them as I sail them out the window on their army parachutes then that's fine. It means my action men don't get damaged and it saves me from having to run downstairs to fetch them. But I get terribly bored when they insist on organizing candle-lit dinners for my most handsome Action Man and a long-haired Barbie of his choice. After the endless dinner finally ends, they insist on putting them to bed so they can have children, which misses the whole point of being an Action Man in the first place.

I now have to share my bedroom with not only the twins but also Brazen Brian – the first nickname he is given by my sisters because he pulls the hair off their dolls. In retaliation, they pull down Brian's pants and titter and scream. Then they whisper to each other in their usual terribly annoying way and giggle so that no one knows what they're talking about.

My other three siblings sleep in the room next to ours and the two latest babies sleep with my parents so that they don't have to get up to calm them.

Anne Montcocq insists on breast-feeding all of us until the milk literally spurts out her nipples. Believe it or not, that actually happens. It's not merely a myth sprung from the feverish imagination of Renaissance painters depicting the origin of the Milky Way.

To avoid too much queueing and thronging in the sitting room, Anne spends most of her day sitting in an armchair like a milk fountain or a home-based Korova Bar - not exactly an advertisement for standard Seventies feminism, but Anne perceives no contradiction.

Some of us are so abundantly breast-fed, our ear-wax and stool have turned white. The little ones have milk dribbling down their nostrils like nosebleeds.

The more my siblings pump up milk, the more our mother's breasts enlarge, producing lactiferous liquid by the gallon. Because of this, she is often in pain in the evenings when the small ones are asleep. She tells her husband that her over-taut breasts feel stuffed with tightly packed milk stones.

In his infinite resourcefulness, Martin Montcocq decides to buy his wife a Philips Manual Comfort Breast Pump in an effort to ease poor Anne's aches and pains. The concept of waste is anathema to our father so to begin with he stores the extra milk in the fridge and the freezer.

Soon enough both the fridge and the freezer are full of frozen breast-milk and so Martin is faced with a difficult choice: throw out the precious milk of human kindness in the gutter, or drink it himself. No one else is very enthusiastic about trying frozen milk popsicles, so Martin decides to transform our mother's vital substance into fresh, creamy yogurt.

He goes into town on his bike and comes back with a cardboard box on his carrier. It's an automatic Yogurt Maker equipped with seven six-ounce glass jars with lids so you can make a different flavor in each jar. You can also control the degree of sourness, determine fat content and thickness. Our father is delighted with the contraption, so mother humors him. She is mostly too exhausted to object.

Martin is all agog at the idea of saving so much money. As you will see, Martin's real middle name is Thrift. He will do anything to avoid throwing something out. Money-grubbing penny-pinching possesses virtually sacramental connotations for our father.

As I opined in the first chapter of this memoir, you could easily argue that this book is a war novel in disguise. Martin Montcocq was born in 1939, a few months before the outbreak of World War II, and this historical fact gives his naturally eccentric personality an even more idiosyncratic inflection.

Martin's parents had it rough during the war, living in a village in Southern France. Our paternal grandfather was forced to steal potatoes to feed the family; our grandmother lost all her teeth by the age of thirty due to malnutrition. Martin came out of his wartime experience as a toddler with a never-flagging sense that his parents deprived themselves of every possible thing so that he and his sister could make it. Although we are never short of money (I even believe we are rich at this point), our father often takes a strange pride in looking as poor as he possibly can, even at work.

This does not mean that he is Molière's Harpagon (the French equivalent of Scrooge) in exile. Our father is not niggardly most of the time. In fact, his presents are invariably over-generous. But he skimps and stints on the little things. One of his mottos is that you save on the small things to afford the much larger ones. This can require wearing the same underpants for two weeks to avoid tiring the engine of the washing machine. If Anne did not impede the zealousness of Martin's love of thrift, the frugal lifestyle would entail the eating of discarded leather shoes and the recycling of urine as a fizzy drink.

So the yogurt experiment is all of a piece with what our father considers the virtuous practice of skimping. We soon set to work making fruit-and-mother yogurt that I and my brothers and sisters are to relish for dessert. It's a lot of fun to begin with and the twins are practically gung-ho with the thrill of creating home-made yogurt out of Mum. All the Barbies and Cindies are made to sit in attendance. Even two of my Action Men are co-opted into attending the confection of mother's yogurt.

When the milk is drawn in excess of our capacity to incorporate that much yogurt, father decides to make cheese. Not just Cottage cheese and Irish Cheddar Cheese but a whole array of smelly, moldy, maggoty Mediterranean cheeses.

Martin buys a book on step-by-step DIY cheese-making and sets up an experimental laboratory in the garage. After much trial and error (mostly error), he manages to compound a passingly good imitation of Gorgonzola, a slightly over-compact version of human Roquefort and a somewhat too messy attempt at Camembert. With time the motherly cheeses, especially the *cendré* ones matured in wood ash, all become acceptable looking, even if the taste is sometimes, let us say, surprising.

Under the new austerity measures, we all have to take cheese sandwiches to school and chomp down stodgy brown bread slices topped with shavings of intimate home-made cheese.

Mercifully, the Irish government unexpectedly introduces free milk in all schools so we are spared the additional equivocal pleasure of sipping mother's milk in front of our unsuspecting classmates. I tremble at the idea that our school friends might discover what our father is up to.

Sif and Deirdre find out that I am terrified of anyone finding out and make the most of it to blackmail me into carrying out all sorts of tasks. In return, they keep mum about Mum.

I later find out that they are actually as terrified as I am about being discovered. When looking for a ruler in their drawers one day, I also find out that they have been hoarding wrapped sandwiches at the bottom of two of their drawers. The stench of the mold is already overpowering but when I open one of the bags, the spoors of mold literally leap out into my eyes and asthma-ravaged lungs.

After sucking repeatedly on my inhaler, I confront them. They freely, and apparently guiltlessly admit they have actually been bumming lunch off their friends and classmates for months. Their blackmail ends but the cheese sandwiches continue to be dispensed to us regularly for another eight years.

There can be no wasting or unequal distribution of food in the household. As a Montcocq child in the post-war 1970s and 80s, you know that you must finish everything on your plate down to the last pea, down to the last crumb, crust, crud or smear of olive oil. You also know that you are being observed and evaluated for wartime qualities such as generosity, fairness and table-manner etiquette. If you attempt to purloin an extra bun or hastily hog the least ancient-looking piece of bread on the breakfast table *smörgåsbord*, you can be sure that the Martin (in cold war mode) has its hawk eyes trained upon you and that even if nothing is said to humiliate you publicly on the spot, your lack of war effort solidarity (and sibling empathy) will be duly noted for further reference. The Martin's estimation of your character will suffer a downgrading slide on the moral scale and it will be used against you in the distribution of pocket-money and in times of querulousness or quarrel.

This is the essence of Martin Montcocq's *mission civilisatrice* and as pre-adult savages there is no escaping any of it. The 1939 perception of children is still very much pre-Enlightenment: children are wild creatures that mostly need straightening out. It is preferable if they remain mute during mealtimes to savor in silence the value of redress. Children are not elfin beings here to add a touch of magic to the harshness of reality. Their value is viewed in their ability to harness their childishness.

Thankfully, when Martin is in 1968 hippy mode and Anne in a state of post-confessional forgiveness (in other words when the stars are properly aligned), there are times when we are also made to feel as wonderful and innocent as blossoming child-flowers. When we are not treated as despicable ingrates, there is a madcap cheeriness in the air. And even at the worst of times, when undergoing secluded penance in a dark cell under the stairs, we are almost always able to squeeze out some joy thanks to the sheer multitude of interactive possibilities in the household. If one of us is subjected to solitary confinement, we find a way of communicating by Morse-code coughing or by exchanging bits of written paper under the door when our parents are safely out of sight.

*

Later on in the year, the Heidi films are released on Irish television. We notice that Heidi too is obliged to eat cheese. The little angel-face with her sheep-curly hair secretly finds its way into my heart. She is really a curly-haired blonder version of myself.

When I confide, Mother tells me that Heidi is an Austrian actress. Her real name is Katia Polletin. It says so in the film credits. But to me this is meaningless. Heidi is not an actress, she is a little girl who has to live with her grandfather up in the Swiss Alps.

But one day, as I am watching telly, the inexplicable, the unexpected happens. I can hardly believe it. Heidi is outclassed, surpassed, overtaken, left by the wayside in sweetness and beauty. In Frankfurt, she encounters the gorgeously tall, long-blonde-haired, exquisitely fine-featured Clara, and my heart breaks in two. I am at once entranced by Clara's ethereal delicateness, moved to compassion by her infirmity, and stricken with guilt at now thinking Heidi stubby and lamb-like by comparison. It is my first taste of treachery.

My friends give up sweets and Mars bars and Barmbrack for Lent; I give up Heidi and Clara. I am too ashamed to admit that I love them. Love is not something you can own up to when you are an eight-year-old Irish boy. The notion is simply too ridiculous for words. I know that I am the only child who has feelings. Other children do not fancy each other, they scoff at the idea. The thought that anyone could fancy something like me does not even enter my mind.

I feel a strange thing in my chest when I see a special girl in Bishopscourt and then see her again the following week. She walks by and I look at her and feel a strange sensation in my head. Another week she looks at me and then I feel another kind of strangeness. We look at each other for weeks, and then I never see her again, and the strangeness goes away without my realizing it.

The year ends in embarrassment when my mother tells me that I am going to have to help more with household chores. At first, I don't see why she is looking so awkward. I'm used to chores, having been brought up from the age of two to fill and empty the dishwasher.

"Look, Olaf, because you're the eldest and because you're a boy, I'm going to ask you to take care of something that's - let's say, it's a little embarrassing, but I'm sure you'll get used to it."

"What is it?"

"Well, it's Liam and Diarmuid. They've got a problem."

"What's the problem?"

"Well – oh, I wish your father would take care of these things! Ok, here it is. I've been with them to the doctor and he says they have to do a certain set of exercises every day."

"You mean like gymnastics?"

"Yes, well, that's actually quite close. I suppose you could call it that. There's certainly stretching involved. Only the difference is they have to pull their skin, not their muscles, if you get my meaning."

"You want me to pinch them?"

"Oh, no, no. They have to pull their own skin back, if you see what I mean."

"What are you talking about, mum?"

"Right, you're right. Let's call a spade a spade. I'm asking you to take care of them because they've got a problem with their foreskin."

"Foreskin?"

"Yes, you know, you had that problem too when you were smaller and I helped you to pull the skin back on your willy."

"You want *me* to do *that?*"

"Well, yes, would you terribly mind? I'm just so busy feeding the little ones and preparing meals, and your father is too busy writing up papers for a series of conferences in Canada and Sweden right now. It would really help us out."

"Wow. Well, ok. So - what do I have to do?"

"It just means that you have to bring them to the bathroom, and get them to pull their foreskin until it rolls back the way it's supposed to."

"Ok, so in the morning then?"

"Any time, really, you just have to do it every day for about a month or two. Until it works."

For the next few weeks, I line up Liam and Diarmuid in the bathroom and have them take out their peckers. I make them pull the skin back and try to avert my eyes while I'm waiting. It's so embarrassing to have to watch them strain the skin back, their faces reddening with the pain and exertion, their eyes sometimes brimming up with tears. Having to remove the tiny pellets of white stuff that gather on the sides under the skin is like watching white maggots squirm and wriggle when you pick up a stone long embedded in the ground.

At table, I tease them about it a little and Frieda and Sophia start laughing so much they splutter and cough and whole peas and bits of white fish come out of their noses.

Margaret Thatcher becomes Britain's first female prime minister. A nudist beach is established in Brighton. The Sony Walkman goes on sale for the first time in Japan. In Greensboro, North Carolina, 5 members of the Communist Workers Party are shot dead and 7 are wounded by a group of Klansmen and neo-Nazis, during a 'Death to the Klan' rally.

Jack Lynch resigns as Taoiseach of the Republic of Ireland; he is succeeded by Charles Haughey. The eradication of the smallpox virus is certified, making smallpox the first of only two human diseases that have been driven to extinction. The Soviet Union invades Afghanistan. Two families flee East Germany by balloon. Rosamund Pike, Claire Danes, James McAvoy, Rosario Dawson bite the air. Mary Pickford, John Wayne and Park Chung-hee bite the dust.

10
Cruelty® and Queueing

Changes to the Swedish Act of Succession make Princess Victoria of Sweden first in line to the throne. Jimmy Carter proclaims a grain embargo against the USSR with the support of the European Commission. The United States severs diplomatic relations with Iran and imposes economic sanctions, following the taking of American hostages.

Jimmy Carter announces that the United States will boycott the 1980 Summer Olympics in Moscow. Zimbabwe gains *de jure* independence from the United Kingdom. Pac-Man is released in Japan. Vigdis Finnbogadottir is elected president of Iceland, making her the first woman democratically elected as head of state.

Time passes to the beat of a local boy banging a ball with a stick. He whacks all day long and stops only for lunch. You can even tell the time by the smack of his ball. You know when it's one o'clock or six o'clock and you can tell that twenty minutes have gone by because he takes impeccably regular pauses. Donal is both afflicted and gifted with what polite adults call Down's syndrome. Thanks to the spirit of Catholic *caritas*, he is an abortion survivor.

The local children, by contrast, call him Donal the Downer.

As you can see from a name like this, the notion of political correctness in Ireland hasn't yet been adopted universally, especially not in the company of the lads. Cruelty® is a registered trademark for boys in my district and a lot of Irish boys in general. The number of ways in which Cruelty® manifests itself in Cork is astonishing.

It is only a good few years later when I spend a month in an Alpine children's resort in the south of France that I realize that Cruelty® is in fact an international company which probably has branches all over the world.

One evening, when we are wandering through the Alps in search of exhaustion and adventure, the boys find a particularly large, expressive-looking toad fast asleep under some leaves. The first thing they think of is how to crush it to death.

I am horrified by the idea, but don't have the courage to stop the rowdiest, coolest, most widely-feared boy from lifting a huge moss-covered stone and dropping it on top of the aestivating amphibian.

Toad slime is splattered all over our bare legs. It feels like the stone has been dropped on my stomach.

Seeing that I am particularly revolted, the Lord-of-the-Flies-boy who drops the stone confides that back home he has done far worse things to toads. He brags that once he made a toad smoke a cigarette until it literally exploded. The glue on its lips can be pressed until no air can come in between the sealed lips and the cigarette so the poor creature just fills up with smoke, starts swelling and swelling until it finally pops. You have to hold on to the lips with your fingers in the final moments or the air just leaks out.

My ninth sibling is born to the first hours of Donal's ball-banging clock. Mother has begun to give birth at home as medical assistance hardly seems necessary. She stays in bed on the last day, a midwife comes in when my father gives her a call, and she's back out again in under twenty minutes. The only scream that leaves the birthing room is the baby's.

When we go in to greet the newborn infant, our mother is propped up in bed holding the freshly squeezed-out little person, looking utterly refreshed herself as if she's just popped out for a yoga class. The latest baby is to be called Aoife, she announces, in honor of her maternal grandmother. That brings the gender ratio in the household to 8:4. The girls are still winning by a wide margin but it doesn't bother most of us, on the contrary. We like the company of women.

The Pleasures of Queueing

But it does bother Brian. Girls irritate him beyond anyone's understanding. He takes one look at new baby Aoife, says 'Huh!' and leaves the room.

Sophia (Child No.5) and Thorsten (Child No.6) are simply delighted. They want to hold the baby and kiss it all the time. Sif and Deirdre smile and coo like mothers as the three toddlers scream round the room.

It's been getting really crowded in the last two years since the last three have started pottering around. I start feeling I'm in one of the Soviet states I've heard about on the radio where you have to queue for everything in front of mostly empty shops. The radio informs us that in Poland people have to queue for sugar, stand in another queue for flour, another one for bread, meat, washing powder, rice, butter, toilet paper, vegetables and so on and so on until you spend all day queueing for necessities. But because it's the country of *Solidarność*, people queue for each other. So, for instance, if there are no more toilet rolls at home on the shelf, you are literally in deep shit, but not if you have asked the neighbor who is queueing for toilet rolls to acquire some for you too. You will be able to barter your sausages for toilet rolls.

Now in Ireland at the time, there is no such queueing. The only time you ever have to queue is if you want to see a really popular film. When *Gandhi* later comes out in 1982, the queue at the Capitol Cineplex stretches half a mile down Washington Street. And that is only because Gandhi is revered as an honorary Catholic saint.

In the Montcocq household, however, I am beginning to experience something of the bane of regular coercive queueing. If you want to pee in the morning, you have to own an ejectable mattress that will propel you fast enough when the alarm clock goes off if you want to reach the toilet first before the stampede queueing starts. And there is no point in setting the alarm clock earlier or lower as Sif and Deirdre and Brian sleep in the same room as me. If I wake up earlier than the alarm, I have to crawl out of bed with the utmost caution as the slightest creak in the floorboards can trigger a massive human avalanche down the stairs.

Brian and I usually brush our teeth on the landing and breakfast is typically eaten on the stairs. The only thing we do not have to queue for is washing the dishes. Sif and Deirdre are particularly virulent when it comes to this and make sure that Brian and I do our fair share.

Sif reminds me that Vigdis Finnbogadottir is now the president of Iceland according to the latest news bulletin and it's only a matter of years before we get a female Irish president.

"But she won't be a Taoiseach, I betcha," parries Brian.

"She could be!" counters Sif.

"Ah, ya bloody Scandinavian wagon. Yur such a wagon."

"Jeez! What are you after calling me? Brian the Fucker!"

"Ah, go fuck a duck, Sifgadottir! It's your bloody turn ta do da dishes. Isn't dat right, Olaf? We didem yesterday."

"That's it, I'm telling Mum about you. You called me a fuckin bitch!"

"Did not! Go on and squeal to Mummy den, ya Swedish piglet."

"I'm not a bloody piglet! I'm older than you are. *Arrête de faire le gros malin ! Comme tu te la pètes !*"

"For Fuck sake, yeez are always at each udder's troats. Take it easy, will ya! *Franchement, vous exagérez !*"

"Ah, shut up, ya fuckin wanker! Yar supposed to be on moy side. Fuckin traitor."

"Fuckin asshole."

"Fucker."

As you can see from this exchange, my siblings and I are not always entirely tender. I realize Brian has become a hate-filled boy. I talk to him about this and he says there are some Fuckers at school who smash his shoulder every time he passes them in the corridor. I promise to look into it as soon as I can. What else are big brothers for? Some violent retaliation will have the added advantage of bolstering my standing with the little ones.

The next day, I go up to the tallest Fucker in the group that Brian points out to me and kick him hard in the shin. I grab the Fucker's head and roar like a lion right next to his ear causing not a little auditory damage that he will suffer from in coming weeks and probably again in old age.

He starts to cry and I tell him not to touch my brother again, or else. I know how to impersonate a hard man as I've had to deal with them myself for years. I add a little of my own feline ferocity (fueled by years of pent-up ultra-violent retaliatory day-dreaming against yobs). From then on until he reaches secondary school, Brian is left alone. Secondary school is to be another kettle of fish for poor woebegone, belligerent Brian.

That is how things are settled in those primary school days. I don't think twice about kicking anyone in the shins or the balls, if he deserves to be deprived of them. I'm not particularly well built but I'm quick, ruthless and my muscles are dense. I can defeat anyone at head-locking, even the eleven-year-olds in sixth class who are two years older. My usual form of attack if insulted is an unforeseen leap to the neck. I wrap all my muscles around the neck in a snake-tight embrace, pull the particular Fucker's head swiftly down to the ground and continue squeezing the neck with all that I've got. It's particularly brutal and exhilarating and leaves your opponent in a state of semi-comatose dizziness.

I don't let go of any given head until it has said "sorry" or "I won't ever do it again". Usually I have to tell them what to say as the head pieces are either too scared or bewildered or half-unconscious for speech. I guide the poor reddened coconut patiently through its contrition, spelling out the words if I need to.

With particularly reluctant Fuckers I sometimes have to knock the head a little on the ground to get the words out, to the kind of iambic pentameter rhythm I've been taught in class when scanning Shakespeare, though I generally attempt this form of violent versification only if it's indoors against the wall-to-wall carpet as blood tends to leak out on cement and that doesn't look too good when you try to explain it to the teachers. There's usually such a crowd gathered round for the scrap though that teachers don't get to see anything until the fight is well over.

Nobody knows it, but secretly I am Kal-El, Superman in disguise, and this makes me tough and invulnerable. Only Kryptonite can harm me, and although we live on the Emerald Isle, I have never come across any.

Apart from that, I am a perfectly nice, normal, nine-year-old boy. I don't really know why I have become this violent when challenged. I just don't suffer fools or Fuckers gladly, having endured their wiles for too long.

The atmosphere in the Republic is a bit tense and maybe that accounts for the plethora of threats and curses. The first hunger strikes are beginning in Northern Ireland and people are getting a bit edgy. But even without these special circumstances, the Irish male is historically touchy about having lost his masculinity to the English. He makes up for it by treating his sons as if they are colonized natives. That's at least what a friend of my father's claims. A slap behind the ear, a cuff to the nose, a hard kick up the coccyx, a fling to the floor. These are pretty common occurrences, at least behind closed doors, and I do witness one father repeatedly kicking his screaming son on the ground one day during the summer holidays. When it happens, forgetting that I am Kal-El, I don't budge, not wanting to be next in line.

Our father never slaps us or even threatens to strike. Since the Swedish have outlawed corporal punishment in the home, he has told my mother not to spank us anymore.

*

In early November, a strange phenomenon occurs that nobody is able to explain.

We begin to discover holes in the house. There are holes in the apples, then holes in the pears, holes in the bananas and potatoes. Then one day there is an orifice in the wall beside the piano and then, an orifice in the fridge.

When three days later, there is a hole in the piano, Anne Montcocq starts to see red. What or who has been doing this? She wants to know. Is it termites or wood lice or what?!

The next day, there's a hole in the front door.

Six Provisional Irish Republican Army prisoners in Maze prison smear fecal matter on the walls of their cell, refuse food and demand status as political prisoners. Margaret Thatcher delivers her famous 'The lady's not for turning' speech.

The African National Congress in South Africa publishes a statement by their imprisoned leader Nelson Mandela. A wave of strikes begins in Poland. *The Empire Strikes Back* is released. Pope John Paul II visits Brazil; 7 people are crushed to death in a crowd.

Terry Fox is forced to end his Marathon of Hope after finding out that the cancer has spread to his lungs. Governor Ronald Reagan of California defeats incumbent Democratic President Jimmy Carter. A record number of viewers tune into the US soap opera Dallas to learn who shot J. R. Ewing.

John Lennon is shot dead outside his apartment in New York. Eva Green, Venus Williams, Jake Gyllenhaal and Ryan Gosling greet the world. John Lennon, Jesse Owens, Jean-Paul Sartre, Alfred Hitchcock, Josip Broz Tito, Peter Sellers, Steve McQueen and Mae West check out.

11
The Moon is Revealed

Chiang Ching (aka Mrs. Mao) is sentenced to death in the People's Republic of China. Ronald Reagan is shot in the chest outside Washington, D.C. Bobby Sands, a Provisional Irish Republican Army member, begins a hunger strike for political status in Long Kesh prison. A fire at the Stardust nightclub in Dublin, in the early hours, kills 48. Rioters in Brixton throw petrol bombs, attack police and loot shops. Bucks Fizz wins the European Song Contest.

This time it is our father who flies into a rage. We discover at breakfast that a second orifice has appeared in the fridge during the night.

The hole is so deep it goes right through to the inside. You can actually put your eye to it and make out some of the dark objects inside. For the average parent, a hole in the fridge would be a discomfiting blot on the domestic landscape; for our father, especially in his latest bout of thriftiness, it is nothing less than horrifying.

"Can you imagine the electricity required to cool down a fridge with a hole in it?"

Our father is wild-eyed with indignation. In normal circumstances, opening the fridge with him watching you from behind is an unnerving, even chilling experience. It's like entering an off-limits danger zone. Once the threshold of the fridge door is breached, you have only so many seconds to retrieve what you need before the radiation level gets too high.

With our father on the watch, there can be no loitering in front of a wide open fridge, no day-dreaming, or forgetting what you were going to get when you opened the fridge in the first place.

Before you unseal the treasure chest of the fridge, you are well advised to wait. Focus in your mind on the object you wish to retrieve, emit hypotheses about where exactly you think it will be. When you place your hand on the handle, concentrate again. Then, with a swift tug, yank the fridge open, make a dash for the estimated location of the object, grab it if you're lucky enough to have located it correctly, close the door as fast as you can. If you follow the procedure, you are relatively safe. If you fail to observe the protocol, all hell can break loose from the sonorous cavern of father-mouth.

If you have forgotten or neglected the approved procedure, you will know about it very quickly. You start to hear a note of nuclear alarm steadily rising in your father's vocal chords after the preliminary warning has been sounded. If the airlock of the fridge is broken for more than three seconds, the oxygen in the room begins to deteriorate.

So, just imagine what a hole in the fridge can do to father-mouth's nerves.

Let us pause for a moment on the inestimable nature of the Montcocq family fridge. The fridge in our house is where our parents place their most valuable stuff, their most prized possessions, and my siblings and I regard it with a certain amount of awe. The fridge is in fact a sort of safe where heirlooms and food jewels are stored for safekeeping. It's a wonder our parents haven't added a padlock to it. In the fridge, our parents conserve all manner of moldy home-made cheeses, some of which are so worn and wizened they're in crumbs. Even the cellophane is growing its own skin of eukaryotic organisms.

Although our parents are definitely guilty of contributing to the world's critical population levels, let it not be said that they failed to do their part to protect bacterial biodiversity. Over the years, several species of micro-organisms are saved from probable extinction in this fridge lab thanks to our parents' reheat cuisine and food storage technology.

The middle compartments of the Montcocq fridge harbor formerly edible, unidentifiable yellowed treasures suspended in marinating floccose solutions, or preserved in what looks like formaldehyde but can't be.

Erstwhile treats lie there bathing in their own semi-comestible sweat. Gluey substances cling to the sides of the jars or slither down as if trying to escape from unbearable surroundings. Other equally succulent items have pride of place on the uppermost rail shelves.

In the lower recesses of the fridge typically lurk two or three saucepans caked with ancient, formerly comestible crud, sheltering gelid dollops of porridge and/or Bronze Age gruel that can be brought back to life and savored felicitously with hot curdled milk and hardened rancid honey.

In the darkened crypt of the lower fridge drawers, under the shelves, prehistoric vegetables fester and fructify, enjoying all the seasonal cycles of nature. When all hope for redemption has left the vegetal matter, it is brought up to be chopped and flavored to taste.

Although eating this refuse is close to the rituals of religious mortification, it's important to realize that our parents actually display (and presumably experience) the symptoms of pleasure while consuming and ingesting it. Perhaps it is mostly because it means that nothing goes to waste (which in itself is a source of infinite satisfaction). But the joy is not purely intellectual and historically induced by the aftermath of WWII. Deirdre, Sif and I also suspect that our parents relish the additional flavors and sensations that accrue with fungus and time.

After finding a second hole in the finely-varnished piano, this time in one of the white keys, mother organizes a domestic line-up of suspects that includes Sif, Deirdre, Brian, Thorsten and me.

Almost half an hour into interrogation, Brian bursts into tears and admits he has been using dad's hand-drill to pierce holes in the house. When he is asked to submit a reason for such unspeakably sinful acts, he shakes his head, bursts out crying again, says he doesn't know, it is fun, he likes making holes.

After a stay in the purgatorial dressing-room slammer under the stairs, Brian is released from detention. Sophia eavesdrops on our parents while they are discussing the matter behind the closed doors of the sitting room. She tells Deirdre and the girls that our parents both agree on one thing: Brian's compulsive hole-drilling is sexual and he needs to get it out of him. Enlightened parental interpretations of children in those days are still in the grips of Freudian psychology.

The next day, Brian becomes Martin Montcocq's DIY apprentice which means he gets to drill holes in all impunity every time our father decides to add another shelf to the house. If any holes appear in the fruit, Brian is forced to eat them, and say two Hail Marys on his knees in front of a portrait of Our Lady of Consolation in the sitting-room. The random holes cease to appear. Just the occasional hole in the bananas.

*

I am now ten years old. The oldest child in the family and the only one with two numbers to my name. My identity, my personhood, is fleshed out to two whole digits. I carry the weight of two numbers in my self.

With ten under my belt, anything is possible. I feel as strong as an ox-blooded man. I can now lift Deirdre and Sif at the same time in my arms. Despite copious remonstrations, they obviously enjoy being squeezed together, squealing and wriggling and giggling.

At school, I arm-wrestle my classmates and some of their older brothers, win a few running medals and a silver medal for staying underwater the second-longest in the class.

Dara Mossgrave is the fastest runner in school so I watch how he places his legs under the desk and imitate the way he walks. When he leaves the school, I beat the second-best runner in the school and become the local Achilles of Saint Finbow's School.

Robert Smith is still the handsomest boy though and all the girls love him enough to etch his name on their pencil cases and several wooden desks. He is also the very first to witness Ruth Kelly's naked bum.

We still play kiss-chase and kiss-or-pain and piggyback battles but there is some much more serious stuff going on with Ruth Kelly. The boys are as excited as piglets whenever her name is evoked though I fail to understand why being exposed to the sight of a backside can procure so much bliss. As far as I am concerned (in those days), a bottom is little more than a flesh-engorged sewer, a place of filth that God in His mercy has hidden from our sight.

One day, to my utter disbelief, someone tells me it is my turn to see Ruth's royal rear. Even I, Olaf Oh-what-a-laugh, am to be honored with the sight of Ruth's pong-releasing pooh-dispenser.

In whinnying whispers and pig grunts, the rules are laid down to me by Robert and the lads. Ruth, it is told, will only perform for one boy at a time. You get about a minute to stare. If you're lucky, you get to stroke it once. Then she pulls up her clothes and you leave. Those are the rules of Ruth's ruthless rear.

When it comes around to my turn, I am mostly disgusted but a little bit curious to see what all the fuss is about. I half expect to see brown stuff come out of her bottom.

How normal is what I am about to see? I don't even know the word normal yet but I can sense its presence at the core of my being.

To see the two livid half-moons of a girl in broad daylight, freely displayed in the open air. Can this actually be possible, can this conceivably be beautiful?

She motions for me to follow and we hide behind the dark massive chestnut tree down by the wall. I look at her, then down at the ground as if she is about to commit an irredeemable act, as if she is going to uncover a cosmically threatening relic that will rip the fabric of the Universe.

Ruthless Ruth suddenly looks slightly downcast. She hesitates. But then, just as I begin to fear she is not going to show me, she turns around.

Instead of witnessing a flesh-cluttered sewer, I am given to behold a wondrously white globe with a deep and yes, eyebrow-raisingly beautiful cleft, all of a scarcely conceivable smoothness and silk-softened puffiness.

The otherworldly Ruth-creature looks around to see if I am aching for the milk of her bejeweled buns.

I like them so much I lose the faculty of speech.

Ruth of the ineffably bottomous beauty looks towards me, Olaf the humble, Olaf the Oh-Laugh.

Invitingly, almost beseechingly, as if to say "Don't you want to touch it? To grasp, to need and to knead and to worry it?" she stares at me.

All I can do is behold, to witness silently in appalled beatitude.

But before I am able to begin to savor this human treasure properly, entirely, Ruthless Ruth pulls up her pants. And the moment is gone, never to return.

To my knowledge, Ruth Kelly never shows her bum again.

I feel I am to blame, as if I have made her feel guilty and ridiculous. This is confirmed to me one day by a reprimanding look and a shove that Robert Smith himself has given me. My guilt is redoubled instantly.

I have to wait another eight endless years before I see such a bedazzling bottom, and get to show my own in exchange.

The wall next to the chestnut tree remains in my memory for years. I dream about it at regular intervals, so tall and unscalable that no one knows what's on the other side. In my dreams, I find myself sitting awkwardly on the top of the wall cap before falling over into the unknown darkness of the other side.

There is everything you can hope for at St Finbow's School. It's small and cozy, the teachers are nice. I am slightly in love with Miss Sweetham. There is a long-jump sand pit we can practice on at the lunch break, there is couch grass to horseplay on, pillars to hide behind, forbidden trees to climb, a little wall for flirting on. It is paradise and when I am forced to leave, it is the end of innocence and all simple pleasures.

My parents want me to join the local community school so that I am properly prepared to enter the menacing world of Secondary School. I am forced to leave St Finbow's and end up in St Columkill's and a totally different realm.

They do play marbles in Columkill's, but there is a mercilessly swift player, also a new boy, who takes the charm out of playing by winning all the marbles with a careless, devil-may-care speed and accuracy that make the other boys, myself included, burningly resent him.

One day, I decide to bring in a plastic turd I have brought back from our summer holiday in England. Before I know it, the turd has been taken from me and no one will say where it is. When the headmaster of Columkill's comes back after the break, he stops suddenly in front of his chair, stares in horror and demands to know who has put this Thing on his chair.

I realize in a moment of absolute dismay that my very lifelike plastic shit is comfortably nestling in the middle of the Head Teacher's Chair. It is the first genuinely Kafkaesque moment in my life, a farcical anticipation of the more serious adult ones to come.

It lasts over half an hour. The class is interrogated, punished, a suspect is whacked on the backside with a ruler, presumably for having defecated on the Seat. He is forced to pick it up with a bag.

When the Head Teacher realizes it is a fake piece of shit, he looks a little relieved and brings the atmosphere of horror down a tone. The real culprit finally owns up and he is even more resoundingly flogged on the backside this time with a cane, despite the fact that he has demonstrably not defecated on the Head Teacher's Royal Rostrum. Under the smarting torture of the chalk-covered yardstick, he releases my name.

Head Teacher's head swivels swiftly in my direction. It gives me a look of horrified surprise. Surprisingly, he fails to flail my flesh or assail my buttocks with a cane. Is it because he considers me French? Is it because I have straw-colored hair? Is it because my eyes are full of innocence? To this day, I am not sure why he doesn't turn his ardor upon me. Does he fear a diplomatic incident with my foreign-born dad? Am I the Head Teacher's secret pet?

At home, the birthrate is rising apace. Our mother has given birth to another set of twins, bringing the total family count to 14. We continue to wonder when they will stop.

Money is getting scarcer so Martin Montcocq begins to filch from public toilets. This marks the end of an era of buying soft, gentle toilet rolls tender to the touch, and does nothing to improve the revenge of the hemorrhoids. In fact, three of my siblings complain of suffering from painfully itchy bum.

The public toilet paper our father manages to pilfer is actually closer to office stationary than it is to standard toilet paper. It comes in ply sheets rather than a roll. Kays Flats they're called, and the name is appropriate. The sheets are as flat and rigid as extra-thin sheets of copper and about as abrasive-looking as the letter K. Cleaning your bottom with one of them is as pleasant and efficient as wiping yourself with the ripped off cover of a woman's glossy magazine.

The cover of the toilet paper box proudly announces that each interleaved sheet is thankfully Guaranteed Irish.

No doubt, this paper is originally designed to deter lengthy toilet occupation, or even entering the toilet in the first place. Rigid and glazed, it feels as if it has been recycled out of a selection of the sleekest hard-cover magazines. If you look at it closely, you can actually see tiny bits of shiny colored paper enmeshed in the grain of the paper under a fine coat of varnish.

It does not enter my mind that I will ever regret the absence of Kays Flats and their "natural, strong, hygienic ply sheets." And yet, that day does come and it is the most humiliating moment in my life.

It happens one day at school as I am writing a history test.

I have revised for it and everything, but for some reason the dates won't come out of my head onto the page and the anxiety this causes turns the contents of my bowels to shitshake.

The pressure on my colon is enormous. My belly feels like an old, splitting dam under water-ton pressure.

I wait for the agony to subside a little and then raise my hand feebly to ask Mr. Callaghan if I can go to the toilet.

This is a risky question during a test, and Mr. Callaghan has been known to refuse requests of this nature.

Mercifully, the Virgin of Consolation hears my prayer and the teacher lets me leave the classroom. When the classroom door is shut painfully behind my back, I manage to make it as far as the corridor, but then the pressure on my cracking bowels grows so unbearable it stops me in my tracks.

I begin to wonder if I am going to make it to the toilet at the far end of the corridor. With careful, laboring steps, I attempt the art of walking, holding myself with one hand against the wall. I feel like my mother looks when she starts to feel the first contractions on the last day just before delivering one of her babies.

I am half way down the corridor when a bursting pain swells against the walls of my insides and I'm certain that I am going to pop like a balloon, emptying my bowels on the floor.

I pant and whimper and thankfully do not have the strength to undo the zipper of my pants in the hall. A burning brown liquid starts searing my sphincter and I try to hold it all in with every last effort. The pain subsides again and I am just grateful that it is easing off and that nobody is there to watch me except the reader. The relief is sweeter than air to a man who is drowning.

I make it to the toilet seat, almost fainting with gratitude and I have just enough time to pull down my pants before my bottom literally explodes letting loose a monochrome Jackson Pollock all over the cubicle.

I am standing there panting and hunched over just savoring the joy of being released from the pain when I realize with a shock that the roll of toilet paper is nowhere to be seen. This is clearly not my luckiest day.

Holding my pants with one hand, I manage to hobble over to the next cubicle, but there is no paper left in that one either, just the bare cardboard roll. The third and last cubicle doesn't even have a toilet roll holder and the flush chain is gone. I shuffle back to the first spattered toilet bowl, lean against the door to consider my art work and the relative merits of Kays Flats.

What would McGuyver or Jim'll Fix It do in this situation? I'm sure it never happens to them. They probably don't even need to go to the toilet. So I sit there and think how the hell I am going to get myself out of this dire diarrhea.

I can't stay here forever. I can't wait for my father to fetch me. There are no public phones in the school. The smart phone hasn't been invented yet. There is no one to help me, and the worst thing that can happen is the teacher comes out to check if something is wrong.

When push comes to shove, I do the only thing I can do, the only practical solution I can think of. I take off my Superman underpants and wipe myself with them, carefully avoiding the superhero logo out of consideration for its holiness.

I wrap the underpants into a discreet enough looking package balled up in my fist and make my way back to the classroom.

Just as I am about to open the door, I realize that I am going to be a laughing stock if I go in holding my Y-fronts in my hand, so I stuff my fist up my jumper and push down the handle of the door. I lower my face and head for my seat as unobtrusively as possible. I am about to sit down when Mr. Callaghan stops me in my tracks.

"What's that under your pullover? Take out your hand! Have you been cheating, Montcocq?"

"It's nothing, Sir. I promise."

"Nothing? I can see you've got something under your jumper. I'm not blind, you know."

"No, really, Sir, I'll tell you about it after class."

"Olaf Montcocq, in the name of the Lord take that hand out immediately!"

At this point, there is no turning back. Every head is raised. This is serious and there's no getting out of it. The teacher has raised his voice and the Lord's name has been invoked. Even the swots have stopped writing. Jackie O'Leary and Caroline O'Grady are holding their breath. The whole class is waiting.

Having no choice, I take out my fist clenched as tightly as possible over the bundle of blue cotton so that no one can guess what I'm holding.

I am praying directly to Jesus at this point that I will not be asked to open my hand.

When he sees the underpants ball in my hand, Mr. Callaghan blanches.

"Sit down and finish your test."

Sweet Jesus, thank you.

*

After months of public toilet-paper, our father's acquisitive propensities begin to veer out of control, apparently as a response to dwindling financial resources. Up to now, Martin Montcocq has just seemed like a disorderly man who doesn't know how to tidy his office. For some unexplainable reason, the arrival of a third set of twins seems to trigger what initially looks like a defense mechanism and he begins to hoard.

When I say hoarding, I don't mean that he hoards anything he can get his hands on. Martin Montcocq is not a hoarder on the scale of the New York Collyer brothers, storing every kind of object, trash and later even excrement. But it is a hoarding disorder nonetheless.

Before the severe hoarding starts, Martin has been nothing more than a careful, if quixotic, collector. Like some sentimental parents, our father collects our milk teeth as they drop one by one; unlike most parents, he also collects our dried-up snot crusts in a small transparent film-roll container, asking us to confect as many as we can. I realize that in creatively inspirational terms, the next best thing to an unhappy childhood is an eccentric one.

The real hoarding begins with reams and reams of photocopies.

Piles and piles of it all over the place. Martin's office in college is so cluttered he generally has to push the door ajar with his shoulder. His office at home starts to look like an abandoned printer's shop. You have to step over and around columns of paper, some of them literally reaching up to the ceiling. The little ones play hide and seek in the recesses of the labyrinth until mother intervenes to stop them because it quickly becomes a danger zone for anyone under one meter tall.

With the occupation of the paper piles also comes the beginning of our father's Rage against the Mess. We begin to hear loudly muttered curses that reveal Martin's cultural character in all its Frenchiness. A recurrent piece of invective is *pute borgne!* which literally means "one-eyed whore." But it is only years later that our father explains the deeper meaning of this. We initially perceive this expletive as *Putttuhborrrn! Putttuhborrrn!* a letter-hoard which signifies nothing but sounds both impressive and daunting. When you hear it explode through the house, you know it is best to stay out of the way.

I have never heard this curse uttered by any other Frenchman. It is one of those old-fashioned expressions like *gourgandine* or *coureuse de rampart* that nobody understands or uses any more in the Francophone world. You must not forget that our father's French has undergone something of a cryogenic conservation. Without being a true-blue archaicist, he is something of a lexical reactionary, a verbal conservationist. Newfangled words hold no interest for Martin and are to be resisted as foul encroachments on the purity of the language of Racine, unless they replace an English loanword. As I have already remarked, Anglo-Saxon loanwords in French are viewed by Martin Montcocq with about as much favor as an English-led incursion onto Gaulish soil.

As the mess in our father's home office grows larger, so too his imprecations gain in length. If he happens to misplace a vital sheet of paper for his students, he begins to inveigh against the entire household, at first cursing the paper piles and pillars, then life on Earth and various members of the family.

Our mother is usually the most frequently blamed target of these diatribes because she is the main buttress against his territorial expansion through the house. The sitting room is for instance totally off-limits as far as mother is concerned, so if she spots a pile of papers discreetly proliferating on the coffee table or behind the couch, she enquires of her personal French Bartleby if he will clear them away.

When he answers impassively that he would prefer not to, she has them removed by one of her children or dumps them back into Martin's office in specific locations she often fails to record, an act of war which is enough to break Bartleby's composure for the day. Especially if it is exam papers or papers he needs for his next lecture.

One day, as we are talking in Bartleby's office, Brian suggests he should make dozens of pigeon holes that he can slip his papers into in an orderly, systematized way. Bartleby thinks about the idea for a moment, considering the possibilities, but argues that some papers could easily be put into two or three different categories and so it couldn't possibly work. But it appeases him somewhat to have this discussion and he responds the next day by building a mezzanine floor behind his desk, with Brian drilling holes for the screws.

Into this mezzanine, Bartleby dumps most of the paper, making the space around his desk look more navigable for a while. But it is in the nature of forests to grow, so the rectangular slices of tree accrue again wherever they can, cluttering and clogging all access to the door.

It doesn't occur to me at the age of ten that perhaps he doesn't need to photocopy all his lectures months in advance for an average of 350 students per class.

It is only much later when I study Latin for a hapless year that I reflect that my parents' proliferating progeny is perhaps not just the product of our mother's Catholic principles but a combination of them with our father's libidinal *abhorret a vacuo*. Like Nature itself, our father abhors a vacuum. You might say that his exponentially growing offspring are really an extension of his hoarding. He cannot abide an empty space so he crowds the house with paper and children.

This is exactly what I begin to feel as I reach my eleventh birthday although I do not formulate it in these terms at the time. I am beginning to feel hemmed in to a slowly but steadily dwindling space. There are now four other kids in my room and I increasingly end up doing my homework on the toilet. And I have to vacate even that humble chair for a sibling all the time.

Over 700 million people watch the Wedding of Charles and Diana Spencer at St Paul's Cathedral in London. Pope John Paul II is shot and nearly killed. Socialist François Mitterrand becomes President of France. MTV is launched. South African troops invade Angola. Simon and Garfunkel perform The Concert in Central Park, a free concert in front of half a million people.

France abolishes capital punishment, and TGV bullet train service begins between Paris and Lyon. Antigua and Barbuda gain independence from the United Kingdom. The Church of England votes to admit women to holy orders. The United States and the Soviet Union begin negotiating intermediate-range nuclear weapon reductions in Europe but the meetings end inconclusively.

Muhammad Ali loses his last-ever fight. Pepsi Cola enters China. Elijah Wood, Joseph Gordon-Levitt, Nathalie Portman, Sienna Miller and Beyoncé breathe in air. Bob Marley, William Saroyan and Nathalie Wood stop inhaling.

12

Doleo Ergo Sum

The population of the People's Republic of China exceeds 1 billion. The first computer virus is created by a fifteen-year-old boy. The prosecution of Howard Brenton's play *The Romans in Britain* falls through. Argentina invades the Falkland Islands. The Provisional IRA detonates two bombs in central London. The first compact discs are released to the public in Germany.

In Florida, Disney World opens the second largest theme park, EPCOT center, to the public. The first emoticons are posted. The leader of Poland's outlawed Solidarity movement, Lech Wałęsa, is released from 11 months of internment near the Soviet border. Michael Jackson releases "Thriller."

Anne Montcocq has her first miscarriage. Our parents do not tell us this at the time but the oldest twins and I notice that her bulging belly slowly begins to deflate without a new arrival in the house. They both look stricken. Martin gazes into space, eats breakfast, goes off to wander in the garden, then comes back to eat a second breakfast in silence without realizing he's had breakfast already. After dinner, he unexpectedly perks up, taking this and the affliction of life in general in his fatalistic stride. On good days, Martin Montcocq is something of a cheerful pessimist; he can transform into a nihilist of Schopenhauer proportions on bad days.

Anne Montcocq, however, looks more and more dejected, taking this setback as a sign of spiritual failure. When we come back from our holidays in France, she cries and cries in front of the ferry, refusing to board it, saying that she doesn't want to go back to Ireland.

We are all frightened by the intensity of her outcry. It feels like a betrayal of everything Irish. Aoife, Ian and Liam weep with her in unison. Our father shakes his wife and takes her in his arms. He screams "Anne! You're frightening the kids!"

Anne Montcocq bravely quietens down, gets ready to face Ireland again and we board the ferry, feed the fish with fourteen hours of intermittent vomiting, and land in Rosslare, County Wexford. The ferry disgorges our over-packed Citroën DS and illegally-full caravan at the back.

To cut the cost of onerous ferry crossings for extended families, our parents make us hide in various parts of the car and the caravan, usually leaving two paid-for, showcased children on the back seat.

We take turns in sitting on the seats, but the option we favor is lying hidden by a blanket under the feet of the two children sitting legally, or in the hollow box-benches of the caravan under apples and oranges and potatoes, or behind the curtain underneath the sink.

The thrill of listening to my father make his jokes to the customs officers as we lie muffled in hiding makes you feel inexpressibly blissful and giddy.

Martin Montcocq loves to take a risk. To the anything-to-declare question, he booms out a cheery "No!" or "Yes! My wife, Officer, is a genius!", or "Yes, my love of Ireland!" or "Lots of drugs and babies!" depending on his mood. "Only a Provisional bomb in the boot! Only a can of worms in the caravan!"

Never such excitement again.

In the first years, when my siblings and I can still fit into small cars, my parents drive a 2CV and a Citroën Diane, two relatively similar vehicles with ultra-fluid suspension that practically tips you out of the car in the sharper bends, making you certain that the whole screeching shebang is going to keel over onto the side and scrape its way flying into the curb, wheels spinning and blood sprayed all over the windscreen. But it never happens.

The Pleasures of Queueing

The Citroën Company is so proud of its lightweight bouncing technology that it holds a sale-boosting annual competition all around the Côte d'Azur to see if anyone can flip over the 2CV. Even at top speed (130 km/h), nobody is able to do it. If you make a sudden full swerve at that velocity, the car is so light it just skids along on the side and comes to an ear-splitting, wobbly stop. Martin tries it several times to win the contest and even once with me strapped in beside him when he knows it's safe.

Our father is as proud of his 2CV as Mr. Citroën Himself. He tells us that the inventor of the model conceived the original prototype in order to be able to wear his top hat while driving only months before the Second World War. He actually went as far as to wall it up in one of his garages so that the Germans wouldn't find it and claim it as a Volkswagen.

When he acquires the Citroën Diane model, Martin Montcocq paints it with the colors of the French flag. Bright primary hues of red, white and blue. Tremendously pleased with this finish, he has Anne's car painted by a professional with a blazing Irish flag. At the top of the flag at the back, above the green, white and gold, he stencils the words THANK GOD FOR IRISH WOMEN!

A little flattered, but mostly displeased, my mother has to drive the graffitied car to her part-time job across the whole of Cork City which makes her look, she complains, like a feminist activist gone crazy, an IRA-sympathizing nationalist, a wild-eyed religious zealot or a Hibernophile lesbian, depending on the way you interpret the caption.

At the back of his own car, in blood-red lettering, Martin writes DOLEO ERGO SUM, his personally devised take on Descartes' famous philosophical dictum. I SUFFER, THEREFORE I AM. It seems like the most appropriate place to blazon the motto as his suffering at that point derives almost exclusively from 2CV maintenance.

Our mother is not excessively pleased either when she has to walk home one day because the steering wheel of her 2CV literally comes off in her hands as she's parking the car.

"Martin, can you imagine if it had happened while I was on the motorway? Or in a roundabout?"

"Anne, please. There are no motorways in Ireland. Dual carriageways are as large as you get in this country. It's probably nothing. Just a screw loose or something. I'll fix it in no time. I can't fathom what you're complaining about. This is nothing compared to the time I had to drive across town to a garage in reverse because the gear lever was jammed."

Admittedly, those 2CV motors are awe-inspiring in a number of respects. Their ability to make our father happy and unhappy in equal measure is one of their most remarkable features. Although he dotes on them, paints, polishes, fingers, washes them at least once a week, and spends an inordinate amount of time in the garage smiling at them, they have the capacity to make him bark and vilipend Saint Christopher (the patron saint of transport) and all the Christian, Greek and Scandinavian gods when both cars refuse to be gunned or push-started at dawn.

The Achilles heel of the two-horse-powered vehicle, our father explains, is that its spark plugs are placed just below the bonnet which means the engine tends to suffer from humidity in the wetter months - that is, most of the twelve months in Ireland.

In our first few years with the 2CVs, we learn to help Martin Montcocq push a bantam-weight car eighty meters up a slope and then push it down as fast as our legs will propel us as our enraged, high-octane, slavering father tries to jump-start the car with one foot on the pedals and the other pushing and stamping the road as the car gains momentum on its way down the hill.

Once we are able to get the cars to start in the morning, they warm up and are generally fine for the day. This, however, does not stop father experimenting further in the art of embarrassment on the roads.

When it's Martin's turn in the rota system organized by a number of parents to bring us and a few of our classmates back to our respective homes, he revs up the engine way beyond the speed limit, cuts the ignition in mid-slope and freewheels the car down as far as it will go, until it falls below 10 miles an hour. All for the sake of saving on petrol. This generally causes him to be beeped and shouted at, to which he invariably answers with a frenetic version of the two-fingered Irish fuck off sign out the window or against the back seat to make sure the indignant honker has seen him. On one of these occasions, he inadvertently rams a finger up the frightened and dilated nostril of one of my classmates cowering on the back seat.

This innovative, cost-effective technique anticipates the automatic motor cutting of the twenty-first-century car by about thirty years and affords our father immense satisfaction.

"All in the name of economy", he smiles back at us modestly, "thriftiness is the mother of invention".

I owe my above-average muscle density to those humid years with the Citroëns. The daily morning struggle with the 2CVs account in no small part for my arm-wrestling prowess at school.

When I'm asked one day how I can be so strong and look scrawny, I modestly reply "car lifting" to the admiration of friends and enemies alike.

After a few years of the caravan and Citroën DS (that sleek-looking giantess that looks like it's been streamlined for space travel), our parents settle for a far less Space Age discolored green mini-bus that allows most of us to sit in at the same time if our mother keeps a baby or three on her lap.

Safety regulations in most of Europe are pretty lax, at least in the minds of our parents. It is only in the less naughty 90s that the whole of Europe starts to follow draconian Scandinavian measures.

When our father's dalliance with Citroën 2CV cars comes to an end, for a while he keeps one hidden from Anne down by the woods. When — a mere three months pregnant — she decides to try cycling on her own from Roscoff, France to Mainz, Germany, glamour camping each night in a one-woman tent on the side of the road, ringing for about five seconds in the evening to reassure us that she's still alive and hasn't been raped (we are not to be worried as she keeps a prophylactic crucifix hanging off the front tent pole), our crackpot father asks us if we would like to turn the sitting room into a drive-in until mother gets back. He proposes to take the 2CV hidden down in the woods, dismantle it discreetly in the evening and reassemble the whole car piece by piece in the sitting room so that we can experience drive-in cinema in front of the TV.

We all go wild at the project and Sif, Grainne and Ian immediately make popcorn for everyone. Our father drives the car back in front of the house and we help him dismantle it and bring all the parts to the sitting room, screw by screw, piece by piece, until the whole 2CV is cannibalized and reassembled inside. Only the engine is left outside in front of the garage like a giant metal heart. Martin removes the clip-on windscreen and we help him settle the television set on the bonnet of the car on top of some books where we can all see it properly. Then we fit ourselves into the car, most of us sitting on someone else's knees, and have TV drive-in dinners for a whole glorious three months until mother returns.

Two days before Anne Montcocq's triumphant return as a now accomplished solo cyclist (who has proven just how muscular Christianity really is), we dismantle the car again, reassemble it in front of the garage, reinsert the engine and drive it back into the forest.

When she is back and we are all seated for tea and sugar-coated apple pie, mother inquires what the strange odor in the sitting room is. It smells like a garage, she claims, but no one else can smell it. My father opens the windows to replenish the air and we titter and prod each other and she gives us her look of amused reprimand. She asks again what we've been up to but she never finds out. We have vowed not to tell and our word is our bond.

As consolation for the final loss of his dream cars, my father starts a collection of 2CV miniatures that we are only allowed to look up at and reverence in a glass case in the bathroom.

ABBA make their final public performance. At the University of Utah, a retired dentist becomes the first person to receive a permanent artificial heart. The first US execution by lethal injection is carried out in Texas. At Greenham Common 30,000 women hold hands to form a human chain.

In a Gallup Poll, 51% of Americans do not accept homosexuality as normal. Time magazine's Man of the Year is given for the first time to a non-human, the computer. Kirsten Dunst, Anne Hathaway and Nicky Minaj see the light of day. *Kein mehr Licht* for Carl Orff, Henry Fonda, Ingrid Bergman, Grace Kelly, Leonid Brezhnev and Arthur Rubinstein.

13

Merry Muck and Confirmation

Nazi war criminal Klaus Barbie is arrested in Bolivia. Björn Borg retires from tennis. Seat belts for front seat passengers become compulsory in the UK. Over 2000 Muslim Bangladeshi are massacred in India during the Assam Agitation. Michael Jackson introduces the Moonwalk. Six men walk underwater across Sydney Harbor in 48 hours. 38 members of the Provisional I.R.A escape from Maze prison. *Return of the Jedi* is released.

As a child of twelve, I go to Catholic catechism and also sing in the Sunday choir of a Church of Ireland cathedral. At the time, I don't realize that a few hundred miles north, I would be running the risk of being knee-capped and crucified for doing the same.

Swinging from Celtic Catholicism to Presbyterian Protestantism and back again in the Republic is as easy as changing your clothes. In Northern Ireland, attempting to settle in a Catholic neighborhood if you're a Protestant (or vice versa) is about as safe as stepping off the footpath for a piss in the mine-filled jungles of Cambodia.

Choir practice at Saint Fin Barre's Cathedral is rigorous in the English style with its long tradition of superlatively demanding choirmasters. We practice four times a week and deliver two services on Sunday to a small but determined congregation.

I rise through the ranks of the choirboys, more out of seniority than by dint of my affinity for choral leadership, and finally end up being Head Choirboy.

I'm not sure if anyone has spotted my flaw, but I don't really know how to deliver the correct pitch of the first note of the hymns, psalms or anthems that we sing and usually end up mouthing the first note, hoping that no-one notices. I rely on the choirboy to my left who has a far more self-assured ability to magically guess the pitch of the first note.

Once I'm in the swing of the action, all goes well. I have a relatively loud, tuneful voice. The whole thing collapses only once in three years, to my utter dismay and the choirmaster's holy horror. On that occasion, the organ note-stutters, rights itself, derails. The choir shuffles out of kilter, crumbles into silence, makes another false start and finally swoops up into the more or less the right tune.

Thankfully for the choirmaster's nerves and the reputation of the choir, my voice begins to croak and then break quite a few months ahead of schedule and I am able to relinquish my role as Head Choirboy and hide my shameful secret in the ranks of the baritones.

Between the morning and the evening services at the Anglican Cathedral, I swing back to Celtic Catholicism for Anne Montcocq's sake. She brings the whole family to the two o'clock mass at the Church of the Real Pleasure just up the road from our house which means that for the best part of four years, I end up going to three religious ceremonies every single Sunday, come rain or shine, hell or high water.

Sunday is the Lord's Day, definitely not my day, especially when I have to do my weekend homework after the evening service at the Cathedral. But I continue to go to the four week-day sessions of choir practice alongside two weekly services because, despite my lack of musical assurance, I do love to sing. More than that, I relish the comradery with the Protestant boys and the horsing around at the breaks. We run all over the churchyard, playing hide and seek behind the tombstones, jumping on top of each other, wrestling, knocking antlers, head-locking, playing choke-your-choirboy, stuffing grass into each other's mouths, ears and noses. One of my best memories is tackling one of the two Head Choirboys on top of a recumbent tombstone as a junior and coming out victorious.

The differences between the Catholic masses and the Protestant services I attend are quite striking even if the contents remain much the same. At the Cathedral, the layers of silence accrue. The notes of our singing echo out through the nave, lodging like music-sparrows in the walls. The small congregation is silent and meditative. The warden is as quiet as a field mouse and the Dean looks like he has never gone for a shit in his life. He seems not to be of this world. His hair is an otherworldly white and his anecdotes make him sound as if he goes back to Heaven every Sunday evening. In fact, we have no idea where he lives. He doesn't bring a car and we never see him arrive. He seems to materialize out of nowhere and disappears after the service before we can spot him walking home.

Mass at the Catholic Church of the Really Cool Pleasure is an entirely different affair. The Priest, Father Judas Croagáin, has the demeanor and the gait of a saliva-dribbling frisky Labrador. To look at him give his sermons is to have the mixed impression that he is entirely unimpeded by brains, and that he is very shrewd in alternation.

Father Croagáin has been to Africa on a five-year mission. You also get the feeling that out in Zimbabwe he was doing more than just helping to evangelize and cure the sick. I don't even know what the rumors are, but you get the distinct sensation that Father Croagáin has had quite a time out there. He comes back ruddy and gay and full of generalized fervor making his sermons closer to stand-up comedy than devotional homilies.

Even at the Eucharist when the wine and host are literally being transformed into the Blood and Body of Christ according to the doctrine of the Catholic sacrament, Father Croagáin looks like he's at the local shopping center trying to peddle a particularly good bargain, as if he's saying "you will find that this exquisitely designed Marks & Spencer Host fits into any type of ice cream."

He is often seen to be grinning or winking (if not practically wanking) at the married ladies at the front, as if to say 'wouldn't you like to roll in bed with a guy like me who knows how to accomplish the Eucharist trick?'

At the sharing of the Host, Father Croagáin frowns on those believers who wish to receive the Host in their palms. He prefers you to close your eyes tight and stick out your tongue, wagging your tail like a puppy.

He always takes his time depositing the wafer on your tongue, has a good long look at the shape and size and texture of it until you feel you're at the dentist's on the point of having a molar pulled out. I have never been to confession with him but I can imagine it's like going into a massage parlor with soft-porn magazines in the waiting room.

The atmosphere in the congregation is equally relaxed, with conversation in full swing at the back and the hard-man teenagers smoking in the aisles, putting in a token appearance so they won't get belted by their old man when they get home.

Everyone goes to mass on Sunday whether they believe in God or not. It's just a thing you do along with eating and sleeping and going to work. At this point in time, Ireland is still under the illusion that all ordained priests are naturally good and that there is a whole world of difference between dipping your fingers in Holy Water and touching the backside of a cow as you leave a Hindu temple.

In a few short years, as Ireland approaches the twenty-first century on the back of Celtic Tiger economics, attendance is about to fall to practically nothing. Mass will get shorter and shorter as the clergy adopts Taylorist motion study to save time in front of newfangled, streamlined, assembly-line altars. Mumble a quick two Hail Marys, get up and down once or twice, shuffle quickly up the line, flick out your tongue, slap on the host and a slice of pickle, shut up your mouth, make room for your neighbor, swallow down quickly and exit the door.

But at this point in time, people still say "hello Father" in the street in a hushed tone of near-erotic reverence, they let the priest skip to the top of the queue, they give vast sums of money in discrete envelopes if a Father visits the house on a casual, money-driven call. They even cross themselves on the bus. At an incomprehensible signal, hands fly up to the forehead like the cheering arms of fans at an American baseball match.

Below a sign that reads LAUS DEO (which Brian says means Lousy God), there's a large worm-eaten wooden statue of Christ at the entrance to the church. Jesus's legs are covered in permanent lipstick stains right up to the knees. If the sculpture had been placed lower down, the lipstick would no doubt reach higher up.

To please my teacher that year I take the pledge during Confirmation. Everyone else is muttering the pledge as part of the effort to foster Irish Temperance so I feel I should do it too. My Class Teacher is looking at me so I say it, I vow not to imbibe any alcohol before the age of 18. The teacher is pleased, I think, although I later get the impression that maybe he is only looking at me to see if I will fall into the trap, and I do.

When I get home and tell my parents I have taken the pledge, my father is furious that his eldest son is not going to take a sip of French wine for six years.

I make up for this pristine behavior, these spotless cassocks and Roman-style surplices, by having messy fun with my siblings in the yard behind our house.

Our own Brother Brian, later to be known as Brian the Sperm for reasons I will disclose in due course, is the officiating presence in the back yard. He is the family Muckrake. By muckrake I do not mean that he is showing early signs of becoming an investigative journalist who will unearth the scandals and secrets of Hidden Dirty Ireland or that he is a Muckrake in the John Bunyan original sense of Sinner but that he begins to manifest a deep affinity for the Irish Mysteries of Mud.

Whenever it rains, which is virtually every day, Brian is out in the garden stirring the mud pit with a stick or his hands. He assembles mudmen and mudwomen, builds tunnels and adobe garages for his miniature cars.

But what he is best at, what he loves to do best, is administer mud baths in what he calls his parlor. For his very willing siblings he confects a smooth admixture of earth, sand and water, smears it on the skin until you are caked from hair to toe in a thick coating of muck.

In time we invite our friends and neighbors along and Brian makes them strip down to their underpants so he can cover them in terrestrial chocolate.

Brian stands decked out in ceremonial regalia. He has acquired an Indian headdress of feathers that drops down to his ankles so he can lord it over the rest of us. At his command, we run around like happy Irish Indians, powpowing and drizzle-dancing and running after each other in a slippery game of catch-as-catch-can.

Brian has a court of squaws that he likes to take special care of, rubbing their thighs and vaginas with thick dark impasto. He ties flowers around their fingers and blows dandelion seed heads over their mud coats as a sign that they now belong to Brian. Ian is his second in command and sometimes gets a share of the brotherly spoils.

This hidden speakeasy palace of mud goes undetected by our neighbors and parents for weeks. On discovery, the place is cordoned off.

When Brian is allowed back into the yard again, none of his neighborly squaws are permitted to come back. But the worst setback for him and for us occurs when it stops raining for an entire two weeks - a record in the history of Irish climatology.

The mud pits in the backyard stiffen into a hieroglyphic scar-tissues of earth. Brian spends his time mulling over the ridges with his stick like a deserted god, scratching away at the dried up cakes and dollops, grinding up pieces into handfuls of mud dust. He makes us dance desperate rain dances until we are tired in the thighs.

"Indians of Ireland! Sing me da songs of de rain! Siobhan! Hot are you doin? I'm not asking for the flayking Moon. Will ya just dance a little bit, for Crysake, what?!"

But when the rain comes back, we have tired of the game and Brian is left alone in the backyard, muttering to himself. It is at this point that he acquires the nickname of Brian the Sperm.

After one of our family field trips to Gougane Barra, he brings back a bucketful of frogspawn. He pours the jelly into one of his mud holes, adds water and grass and some of the duckweed he brings back from the trip.

He tends the frogspawn into tadpoles and frogs and then builds a cage so the frogs can't get out. Half the backyard becomes a frog conservatory littered with potholefuls of frogpawn and tadpoles and trapped croaking stud frogs.

When later that year, Brian starts digging trenches in the garden and begins to enact First World War scenes of distress, mother intervenes, blames our father for the war atmosphere, and has us fill up all holes and trenches. The garden is now off limits for all of us and our parents decide to grow a large kitchen garden to keep us off the territory.

And then one night, Aoife and Liam see Brian stealing down to the yard in his birthday suit to toss the turkey over the sprouting potatoes and leeks.

A few weeks later, our mother comes in asking where all the cloth handkerchiefs are. Is the washing machine gobbling them up or is someone squirrelling them under a pillow? There are practically none left and Thorsten has a cold. Can whoever has the handkerchiefs please hand them back?

We only find out where they've gone to when Sif wakes up in the middle of the night to the sound of groaning and a watery clop-clap-clap-clapping under Brian's bedclothes.

Finally, there's a longer moan and Brian's tossing blanket subsides into silence. Sif sees an arm stick out of the bedclothes. It hastily stuffs a bunched up embroidered textile tissue under the rim of the bed.

The next day, rummaging under Brian's bed, we find 47 family-heirloom handkerchiefs, embroidered with our mother's maiden name initials, hardened and yellowed with what smells like congealed semen.

We chuck them in the washing machine, spin a cycle at 90 degrees and present them to Mother saying with a tongue-in-cheek smile that we don't know where they came from, we just mislaid them someplace. Brian gets away with it and we buy him a box of paper tissues but the name Brian the Sperm sticks to him adhesively until the day he leaves home.

All in all, we are the happiest and most fully functional dysfunctional family I know. Totally and felicitously dysfunctional.

Soviet military officer Stanislav Petrov avoids a nuclear war by correctly identifying an American nuclear missile attack as a false alarm. South Africa approves a constitution granting limited rights to Coloreds and Asians. The Turkish part of Cyprus declares independence. A Provisional I.R.A bomb kills 6 Christmas shoppers and injures 90 outside Harrods in London.

Brunei receives independence from Britain. Bombs explode in Paris and Marseille. McDonald's introduces McNuggets. Emily Blunt, Chris Hemsworth, Jesse Eisenberg and Jonah Hill open their eyes. Tennessee Williams, Rebecca West, Hergé and Joan Miro close theirs.

14

Incest and School

Medicare comes into effect in Australia. The UK miners' strikes begin. Sinn Féin's Gerry Adams and three others are seriously injured in an attack launched by the Ulster Volunteer Force. Marvin Gaye is shot to death by his father for his birthday. Ronald Reagan calls for an international ban on chemical weapons.

English comedian Tommy Cooper has a massive heart attack and dies live on TV. The United States announces their discovery of AIDS. The Soviet Union announces that it will boycott the Summer Olympic Games in Los Angeles. Ronald Reagan visits his ancestors' house in Ballyporeen, Ireland. A Soviet submarine reaches a record submergence depth of over 1000 meters.

In the year of Orwell, the clocks strike thirteen and I enter the big brotherly world of Secondary School. There is even a school called Christian Big Brothers, but that, thankfully, is not the one I am sent to.

We no longer have a single stable teacher but many different teachers. The geography teacher's bottom wiggles a lot when she writes on the blackboard. The math teacher has a foxy version of Karl Marx's beard. My classmates call him Fungus.

Our Irish teacher gives you the impression that her mouth secretes honey rather than saliva. She makes us recite Hail Mary Full of Grace in Gaelic with our hands joined in front, even though we're supposed to be the only non-denominational school in the city. The principal turns a blind Catholic eye. It is not in our best interests to complain and no one could be bothered to anyway. I don't learn what a Muslim is until the age of 18 and for a long time I think that Jew is the little drops of water that are deposited on the lawn in the morning.

The French teacher relieves my boredom by being unbelievably gorgeous for someone that old. She has a massive nest of hair and wears glamorous, Hollywood-style lipstick. The history teacher feels it is sufficient for us to learn about no more than a hundred years of Irish history until we leave school. Why bother with such niggling details as antiquity, the middle ages, the renaissance and two world wars when you can focus for five years on the charisma of Charles Stuart Parnell, the 1916 Rising and the Irish Civil War?

English is my favorite subject despite the fact that we have to read the stuff written by a dead blind poet, another poet who thinks gardens are better than people, a novel about an old guy who goes fishing and comes back with the clothes practically eaten off his back, and an even stranger play about a man who agrees to have a pound of ham sliced off his chest.

I learn about what petty cash is and how to fill in a check in commerce class, about chemical compounds in science and how to draw an equilateral triangle in mechanical drawing.

Although this is all new and surprising, one day, Deirdre, second sibling in command, comes to inform me of a secret that is to change the way I perceive human customs, not to say life on Earth, in a far more challenging way.

"Olaf, I have to tell you something I can't tell mum and dad. The two of us have to sort out the problem."

Deirdre has always been the picture of demure common sense, the paragon of Irish virtue, the one of the Righteous Path. She is the most Irish of all of us, the least French, surpassing even mother who has become Frenchified through repeated intercourse since the invasion of our strange Norman father.

Deirdre looks at me with uncommon intensity but keeps her lips tightly shut. I can tell that what she has to say is having a considerable impact on the Righteous Path that she follows. She has come to an unforeseeable forking in the road.

"What is it, Deirdre? Stop looking as if you've been bitten by a snake. You're making me nervous."

"Well, you could say I have been actually."

"What?"

"Bitten by a snake."

She crosses her arms, sighs, turns her mouth to the side and looks as if she is considering the options and finally says,

"It's about the twins."

"Which ones?"

"The second ones. I'm not talking about me and Sif or the bloody toddlers. I mean Søren and Siobhan."

Deirdre never uses curse words or blasphemy so this has to be pretty serious. She now has my full, undivided attention.

"Sophia saw them carrying on."

"What do you mean by carrying on?"

"You know what I mean. Oh come on! Do I really have to spell it out?"

"Carrying on. You mean - ?"

"Yeah, Una says that she caught Siobhan pulling away at Søren's -"

"Søren's?"

"Søren's - willy."

"You mean as in she was pulling him?"

"Yeah, I think you get the flaming picture."

"Ok. Well, what do you want me to do about it?"

"Well you're the oldest. You should know. Give them a telling off! Tell them you'll squeal on them. Tell them no bloody television until Christmas! How should I know?"

"I can't stop them watching telly. Mum decides that."

"Well then make them stop any way you want to. We can't have them carrying on in our house. Think of what the Bishop would say if he found out!"

"Deirdre, how would the blinking Bishop find out about something like that? They'll probably grow out of it. It's just a game, I'm sure. They're hardly going to be doing it every day."

"Look, if you don't talk to them, I will, ok?"

"Ok, ok, I'll look in to it. Calm down, will you? I'll tell them this evening. I'll wait till they've switched off the light."

When I go and see them that night, they are whispering in the lamppost-lit twilight of the bedroom. Siobhan is smiling down excitedly with her overlarge gapped new teeth at Søren who is gazing up at her in beatitude. His mouth is also full of outsized giant adult teeth. Siobhan is out of her bedclothes and has her hands and a foot on the ladder that leads down to the lower bunk.

"Get back into bed, Siobh, you're supposed to be sleeping."

"Go to bed yourself, Olf. You're supposed to knock on the door, don't you know basic manners?"

"Look who's talking. I don't think I've ever heard you knock on a door before."

"Whatchya want?"

"Nothing. I'm just checking in on you."

"Well, we're fine. Gnight."

"Listen, Deirdre's been telling me you need to take it easy."

"Take it easy yarself."

"She says..."

"Wha?"

"She says you're..."

"Olaf, would ya ever get lost? We're supposed ta be sleeping!"

"Alright, alright, that's exactly my point. I'll see ye tomorrow. Good night. Just stay in yer own bunk, right?"

"Erra, mind yar own business."

As you can see, I'm not exactly an authority figure for my siblings. I go back to the room I share with Deirdre, Sif, Brian and Thorsten. They're talking in hushed tones and interrupt their conversation when I enter.

"So? What did they say?"

"Yeah, I told them. They didn't really seem to know what I was talking about. I'm sure they've probably forgotten already."

"Olaf, I seriously doubt it. I just can't imagine myself going to mass with this on my conscience."

"For God's sake, Deirdre, would you ever cop on?"

I forget about it for weeks and the problem just seems to go away until one day Brian comes to whisper in my ear at the lunch break. The twins have been at it again.

After school, I go over to Saint Patrick's Primary School to pick them up and spot them walking over the green hand in hand.

"Hey, twins! Slow down, I'm walking yeez home!"

"Says who? Can't ya walk yar own way? We don't need to be babysitted you know."

They both look at me with the same stern-cute expression. Their small mouths full of overlarge adult teeth.

"Just thought I'd keep you company. You look a bit lonely all by yourselves, and ya never know. A wolf could catch ya!"

I give them both a growl and a tickle but Søren kicks my shin and Siobhan dodges my hands, casts her eyes up to heaven and sighs like a child-weary mother.

"Fuck off, Olf, we're not inta tickling anymore."

"Ok, alright, I'm just fooling. You're all so grown up! Jesus, what happened to fun?"

"Oh, we have lots of fun. You're the one who's always bored with everything. Brian says you refuse to play action man with him. And Daredra and Sef say yer always trying to push dem out of de room ta read books."

"Well, I have to do my homework, and I'm thirteen, not exactly action-man age anymore."

"She says you read books that aren't even de ones yar supposed to be reading for school."

"How would she know?"

"Daredra knows everything. She's smarter den you. So is Sef, actually."

"Says who?"

"Says Mum and Dad. We heard em talkin aboud itt on Friday."

"That doesn't mean it's true."

"Of course, it's true. They've always had better marks den you."

"So what? I'm better at English than they are."

"*Et elles, elles parlent mieux français que toi.*"

"Why are you switching to French? Dad isn't even home."

"*Parce que toi, tu sais pas parler français et Papa il dit qu'en plus tu fais plein de fautes quand t'écris.*"

"Listen, you don't even know how to write any language so shut up!"

"*Casse-toi, Olaf, tu pues! T'as qu'à te laver les aisselles!*"

"I swear, if you talk to me like that again, I'll tell mum what you're up to!"

"Hot are you talkin about?"

"You know very well. You were seen touching each other's private parts!"

"Olf. Dat is nun of your business. We shouldn't even be talkin about it."

"What do you mean it's none of my business? Do you have any idea what this is doing to the family? Deirdre is going crazy. Do you want her to lose faith?"

"I don't see that Daredra believing in God or Ronald McDonald has anyting to do wid us."

"Look, what you are doing is called Incest, ok, and it's Wrong. You're not supposed to do it. It's against the law, right. No one does it, like. It's just not natural, ok?"

"We know what incest is, Olf. It's only a word."

"You're just unreal, you know. The two of you. You sound like a two-headed anthropologist. Why can't you just be two normal kids? Normal, identical siblings who quarrel and backstab and hate each other's guts?"

"We hate you and Daredra and Brian de sperm a lot of de time."

"This isn't about Deirdre and Brian and me, this is about the two of you. You just can't go on like this. It can't be done, ok?"

"Well, we're doing it and it's fine."

"You're so unbelievably rational, or just nuts, I'm not sure! I'm telling you, you're abnormal. Look, it's not only illegal, it's against God's plan. The proof is you can't have babies when it's incest. Or if you have them, they turn out like Brian, ok? No, look, this is serious, I mean it. Incest means monster babies that look like this and chase after you like little Frankensteins."

"That's ok, we don't want babies anyway. We have too many at home as it is, doancha agree?"

"What I mean is, nobody will let you do this. You can't get married. People won't let you live together. You'll be branded. People will point at you and say look, they're the monster Montcocq kids."

"Look, Olef, I don't know why you're getting so hott and boddered about itt. We're not doing much, anyway, and we're almost ten. We're old and we're free ta do what we want. This is a free fuckin cuntry."

"Jesus, Siobh, I swear you've been watching too much American television. Get real, will ya? I promise, if I see you or anyone else sees you so much as kissing, I'll go straight to Mum and you can bet that she will do sometin pretty drastic about this, like putting one of you up for adoption."

"If you do that, we'll elope."

"Elope! Would you listen to yourselves? Ten-year-olds don't elope! Ten-year-olds steal sweets from shops, they tell white lies, they play hide-and-seek, at most they play kiss-chase with kids outside the family!"

"We do that too. Just leave us alone. We love each udder and dat's itt. No one else will be closer than we are. No udder friend will ever know me or Siobhan better. You can't understand, Ok, because you don't have a twin and even if ya did ya still probably wouldn't understand. Now, could ya please leave us de fuck alone!"

The Provisional I.R.A attempts to blow up Margaret Thatcher and the British Cabinet in the Brighton Hotel. A million people die of starvation in Ethiopia. Directed by Bob Geldof, Bandaid records "Do They Know It's Christmas?" The Timil Tigers begin to massacre Sri Lanka. Relations between Somalia and Kenya improve. The Crack Epidemic begins. Paul Dana, Katy Perry, Mark Zuckerberg and Scarlett Johansson leave their mother's respective wombs. Yuri Andropov, John Betjeman and Indira Gandhi are placed in the Earth and the Ganges.

15

The Year of the Flea

Greenland leaves the European Union. British Telecom withdraws its red telephone booths. The border between Gibraltar and Spain is reopened. A Beirut car bomb kills more than 80. South Africa ends its ban on interracial marriage. Scientists in Antartica discover a hole in the Ozone. Josef Mengele's remains are discovered in Brazil. Bangladesh is hit by a tropical cyclone that kills 10,000. Route 66 is officially decommissioned. Air India Flight 182 blows up above southern Ireland.

Mother's latest baby accedes to full family membership. It's a girl yet again, which leaves the males of the tribe at an irrecoverable disadvantage. Girls 10; Boys 7.

The girls are gloating, but we guys remain pretty serene. Brian is so hyperactive he counts for three and our father is eccentric enough for five fathers.

Martin Montcocq gives us his half-crazed fatherly smile of reassurance. Owen lets out a Whitmanian yawp and the incestuous twins look on in owlish silence. Deirdre, Sif and Una say they are going out to see *Cocoon* at the Capitol with some friends.

The smallest twins are cuter than ever, running and tottering, banging into walls, knocking over glasses of milk, smashing into bottles, recklessly sticking their heads for interminable seconds in the fridge when our father's not looking.

I ask them things like what are clouds made of. They stare and hem and haw a little and then they say "it's, it's, it's smoke, it's smoke dat gets caught on de sky." When I tell them that's not true, they say "de clouds, it's, dat's, it's candy floss dat, em, dat, em, dat floats up. Like bloons. Like balloons, like."

"So why are some of them grey, almost black?"

"Der black because, because, because... Der black, der grey because der dirty. You need ta hoover de dark wans."

The next day they instruct me that you can just punch two holes into a bin or a wall and plug in a lamp to access electricity.

One of them calls me "cutie-beauty", which is terribly endearing coming from so small a person, even if he's only repeating what I say.

I have a lot of fun teasing all sorts of strange ideas out of them that they don't remember later.

Our father's hoarding is hitting a peak. He is beginning to extend the range of his interests in found objects, bringing back all manner of unusual, pointless bric-a-brac. Curiosities that could serve as decorative ornaments but don't, oddments that might one day come in handy but ultimately never do, building materials of all shapes and sizes, odds and ends you wouldn't believe. There is so much fatherly clutter that it's beginning to overlay Anne Montcocq's religious pictures and knickknacks. The main Wailing Wall is sealed up by a second layer of bookshelves.

Martin's office is now completely crowded out and the front and back gardens look like fully-fledged junk yards. He keeps trying to make incursions into various other rooms in the house but these are forcefully rebuffed by Anne Montcocq. He gets into arguments with Sif, Siobhan and Diarmuid when he tries to sneak some of his papers onto their desks. The smaller siblings don't have desks yet so Deirdre, Brian, Thorsten and I have taken to locking our room and bringing the key to school so he can't get in and start piling reams of paper or building extra shelves to the ceiling.

In an effort to keep the extent of the clutter in check, Martin Montcocq tries to atone by erecting a scaffolding of shelves against every available wall space and even over shelves that are already there. While this does tend to reduce the ground surface mess, it also makes the house look stuffier and smaller. We all feel the walls are closing in, but Martin argues that books make for excellent insulation, that soon we won't have to put on the heating in winter. As an experiment, he decides to cut the central heating and we end up spending the winter months shivering under an increasingly acarid-filled, asthma-inducing *millefeuille* of blankets and quilts.

When I claim that some of the books are starting to smell of must and look mildewed, Martin blows his top, retorting that we are always complaining. I back off as usual, lamely muttering that he doesn't even read the books he owns. He turns a deaf ear to this and continues lamenting the fact that there is nowhere for him to settle and that if we could hound him out of the house with cockroach spray we would do it.

A reverse version of these prophetic words almost comes true three weeks later when one of the three stray cats Martin brings back as a television-room soother begins to infest the house with its fleas. Unaccountably, the whole family except thick-skinned Martin is bitten in every conceivable place.

We have to spend our time changing clothes, casting them hastily into bin bags, shaking out a cloud of powdery green pesticide into the bags, trying to get as much of it into the bags and not too much in our lungs. We scrub our skins under the shower, examining each other's hides with increasing paranoia. The bedclothes have to be renewed at least twice a day, monitored, powdered, quarantined in bags and washed at high temperatures.

After two weeks of this, we are so sick of the rigmarole that we actually consider leaving the house for a while and going to a hotel in town to get some respite in the vain hope that the fleas will die of starvation if we remove both ourselves and the cats. Our mother's usual Martin-inspired penny-pinching defenses are down and she's ready to go but father's Second World War citizen effort sense of thrift rises up in opposition at the wasteful cost.

His usual answer to everything is "I'll look it up in the library and then we'll know what to do."

Strange to say, our father never gets bitten, which makes him barely give any credit to what he perceives as our collective fantasy that the cat has infected the house with fleas, even when we show him proof of scratched, swollen bites, so many of them that it's beginning to look like we have measles.

The Pleasures of Queueing

Martin Montcocq belongs to the oxymoronic category of what one might call Modern Medieval Man, a kind of paradoxical Atheist-Creationist Darwinist. He knows that germs and carbon dioxide are provable facts but subconsciously feels that what you can't see doesn't really exist. Smells, for instance, just smell. They are not caused by chemical substances released by bacteria. He will tell you there's no way that God created the Earth but at the same time he can't really abide by the theory that the oceans and seas are most likely the result of repeated frozen meteorite bombardment over millions of years.

A few hours later, he comes back from the University library looking considerably cheered. Here is a rough translation of the conversation:

"Right, everyone! Family meeting! I've got the solution to your troubles. Everyone come down to the kitchen. Speaking panel! Roundtable discussion!"

"What is it, Dad? What did it say?"

"Sit down everyone, I can't speak before you're seated and attentive. There's a chair over here. Here, you take that one. Ok everybody, I think I have a solution. But first, let me fill you in on a few enlightening facts. Sophia, are you listening? Søren, Siobhan, stop looking at each other for a minute. I need you to concentrate. Emil, please stop eating your snot crusts. You should have stopped that by now. Hasn't he had enough breakfast? Anne, tell him to stop. Look, I'm not going to talk unless you're all listening properly. Can someone tell me why there's a baby under the table? Is that Samuel or Ian? Anne, please. Right. Now. Let me fill you in on what I've learned. First things first, I think that I have identified the genus of the insect. The flea that you claim to be plagued with goes by the name of *ctenocephalides felis*. That is, if it is cat fleas that you are afflicted with. If we are talking about the human flea, which in my opinion is the case here - assuming that you have them at all - then it is known as *pulex irritans*, so called because it's a bit of an irritant of course. The feline flea is reddish-brown, hard as an armored vehicle. It possesses exceptionally powerful hind legs that -"

"Dad."

"Yes?"

"You're giving us a lecture."

"Well, don't you want to hear all there is to know about the source of everyone's complaints for the last three bloody weeks? I think I'm entitled to a little leeway here considering that I went to the trouble of looking this up for you. Una, why are you eating that toast with the jam on the wrong side of the bread? It's just going to drop off onto your blouse. You know that don't you?"

"It's because she wants the jam directly on her tongue. Liam does it too."

"This family is crazy."

"Dad."

"Dad! We want to know how to get RID of them."

"Yes, well, I'm coming to that. If you could only show a LITTLE patience."

At this point, my mother starts to rustle her plastic bags. This is an activity that Anne relishes. It's a frequent background noise we only notice because it wracks our father's nerves to an amazing degree. He takes it as a form of domestic torture that is to be endured at best in tense silence, as he concentrates on mastering the pain being inflicted on the receptors in his ears.

Martin stops talking, waiting in pained silence. If the rustling goes on for too long, he usually gasps for Anne to stop.

Anne Montcocq continues to rustle the large collection of plastic bags squeezed in between the dishwasher and the wall. She is looking for the perfect bag. We sometimes wonder if she realizes the strain and pain she is inflicting or if she does it on purpose.

"Ok, let's get on with it! Let dad speak or we'll be here all day. Come on, Mum, release him."

"Anne, would you mind stopping that for a second? I can't get my thoughts into shape."

"Dad, don't mind her. You know she won't stop until she's finished."

"I'm looking for a bag, can't you see?"

"Ok, ok, ok. Can't you just take the first one that comes to hand?"

"Just a second. I need one that's the right size and strength."

A little more pained silence ensues, even though the rustling has stopped, as our father's nerves recover from torture.

The Pleasures of Queueing

"Thank you for your undivided attention. As I was saying then, the fleas you claim to be infested with are the best jumpers known to man after the froghopper. The latest finds suggest that they do not use muscle power but energy stored up in a protein called resilin. As you know, they live by hematophagy, which means that they basically eat your blood."

"Eat your blood? Yuk!"

"Uuugh!"

"Yocky!"

"Pooh!"

"Dat's so gross."

"Yes, admittedly, it does sound disgusting. I will grant you that."

"Yok!"

"You may be surprised to hear that they live up to 100 days and that the female lays up to 5000 eggs in its lifespan. It also came as a surprise to me that the adult flea accounts for only an estimated 5% of the whole flea population. Hence our problem: the larvae live on after the parents have gone. Ah, yes, and do you know another thing? The larvae eat the parents' fecal matter. Their caca."

"Yuck again!"

"You'd love that, wouldn't you, dad? Really cheap food and straight from the heart."

"Well, you know I'm a pelican."

"Solution, dad..."

"So, yes, the solution. Well, I think I may have it. Now, the first thing to do, if you are able to catch a flea, is to roll it."

"Roll it?"

Anne Montcocq starts to rustle amongst the bags again.

"Please, Anne. My nerves."

"Mum!"

Anne stops moving, her hands still in the bags.

"Yes, you have to roll them between your fingers, because if you try to crush them, they just spring out of your hand. Remember, the flea's shell is extremely resistant to pressure."

"Martin..."

"Yes, dear?"

"None of us has ever seen one yet, let alone caught one."

"Precisely! That's why I'm not sure you have fleas. Maybe you just have measles or chicken pox, or small pox."

"Dad, they're flea-bites, ok? The bites are always in twos or threes."

"Yes, well, admittedly that does sound like flea bites. They always appear in clusters apparently."

"Dad, is it true they give you AIDS? Someone told Oisin they spread AIDS if you're bitten."

"Well, according to a colleague I also consulted at the biology department, it's believed by the scientific community that fleas do not carry or transmit AIDS. The amount of blood they absorb appears to be insufficient."

"Well, that's a relief."

"Yes dear, it certainly is. However, they do act as a vector for myxomatosis, endemic typhus and bubonic plague."

"Thanks for sharing that, dad. That's really comforting."

"I hasten to add that none of these diseases occur in Europe anymore."

"Thanks, dad, you really know how to cheer us up. Do you think we could get to the solution now?"

"The solution, yes. Now, as I was saying, the best way to dispatch a flea is to roll it to and fro between your fingers so that the more fragile legs are maimed in the process. It's as simple as that. The fleas die when they're deprived of their legs."

"Dad, we can't catch any fleas! We can't even see them. Even Thorsten hasn't been able to locate one and he's the Sherlock Holmes of bacteria."

"Ok, ok. Well that brings us to solution number two: the vacuum cleaner. You vacuum them up and apparently it gets 100% of the eggs and pupa and 96% of the adults."

"That leaves us with 4% of the biting adults."

"Yes, but it's a good start, isn't it?"

"How are we going to get rid of the last 4% if they reproduce every ten seconds?"

"They don't reproduce every ten seconds and anyway there are further solutions. I've looked into this thoroughly. There are adulticides for instance."

"Adulticides?"

"Mature flea-killing powders. If the adult fleas die, they can't reproduce and the race goes extinct. There's also sodium borate, baking powder and other dehumidifiers that dry up the humidity-loving flea."

"Martin?"

"Yes, dear."

"Can I remove my hands from the bags now?"

"Yes, dear. I'm leaving the room. Just wait a second."

"I'm feeling really nauseous."

"Oh, yes, of course! Deirdre, Sif, Olaf, get your mother a basin!"

"It's ok, Martin. I've found the right bag."

In the end, we're all so desperate that we try all of Dad's solutions. They work for a while but the fleas seem to cocoon and come back with a vengeance two months later. This time, Thorsten manages to capture a flea in the hem of a blanket and proceeds to carry out a series of experiments on the unsuspecting flea. It dies in his hands under torture.

Three days later, he catches another one and wants to start a flea circus. He actually manages to tie a piece of thread around its head as a harness and ties the other end to a threaded ball of paper. We watch it hop around with its ball and chain and hope it will lead us to its people but it just bounces around the place and we don't get any the wiser but we do have a pretty good laugh.

We try Dad's solutions again and again, and finally one day mother is sick of it and calls Pest Control when Dad is at work. They come and spray DDT, a toxic substance scarcely less dangerous than Agent Orange, our father informs us, when he comes back in the evening and finds out.

Three men come in wearing masks and pink plastic gloves. They spray the fur on all three cats, on all the wall-to-wall carpets and rugs and tell us to leave the house for a few hours if we can and not to touch the cats or the carpet.

That evening no one complains of any extra bites and we gather in the sitting room to celebrate the end of the Alien invasion. My father reads us an extract from Albert Camus's *La Peste* in a deeply dramatic voice and we laugh ourselves under the table with hilarity and relief.

When the cat suspect No.1 comes in to see what all the ruckus is about, we fall quiet and eye it with the suspicion it probably deserves. Everyone except Dad votes to have the cats stay out in the garden.

When all is said and done, it is our father's reading of Camus and the experience of enduring fleas that make me want to become a writer. Writing seems like the perfect way of turning bad into good, pain into pleasure, weariness into wonder, a way of transmuting shit into gold when shit happens as it inevitably does.

The only difficulty with writing in the house is that it's practically impossible to get more than a few lines onto the page before being disturbed by siblings or parents or untimely erections. I spend the next decade struggling for silence, grappling with thoughts that churn in my head like dirty clothes in a washing machine. My undiagnosed attention deficit disorder is sometimes unbearably hard to get under control. Even in rare moments of almost complete silence at two in the morning, trying to concentrate on a sentence is about as hard as trying to breathe under water.

The rest of the time, which is most of the time, I also have to contend with the constant noises of shouting, screaming, chattering, stomping, stampeding, jumping, frolicking, banging, knocking, hammering, sawing, drilling, coughing and snoring. Oh to concentrate long enough to be able to finish a short story.

Ronald Reagan sells his autobiography rights to Random House for 3 million dollars. The first schoolteacher ever to go up into space boards the Challenger Space Vessel. The Night Stalker is captured in Los Angeles. The wreck of the Titanic is located. An earthquake in Mexico kills 10,000. The Brixton race riots begin. *Back to the Future* is released in cinemas worldwide. Carey Mulligan, Lana Del Rey and Amanda Seyfried enter the stage. Exit Marc Chagall and Orson Welles.

16

Shampoo, Love & Grease

Halley's Comet traverses the solar system for the second time in the twentieth century. Swedish Prime Minister Olof Palme is shot dead on his way home from the cinema. Hailstones weighing 1kg fall on Bangladesh killing 90.

The Chernobyl disaster kills over 4000 people in Ukraine and infects the whole of the northern hemisphere. Hands across America: 5 million people hold hands from New York to Long Beach, California, to raise money for the hungry and homeless. Nick Roeg's *The Castaway* is released in cinemas.

It is spring, the birds are twitching their feathers amongst the leaves, purple crocuses are pushing out radioactive petals all over Ireland. Once again, April is the cruelest. Brian, Sif, Deirdre and I cycle home cheerfully through Chernobylian rain without realizing we're being infected. Little do we know that 21 years later, this gentle ride through drizzle will give Sif and Deirdre thyroid cancer and Brian and me a chronic inability to regulate our body temperature.

My parents have decided to send me away for a year to my uncle and aunt in the South of France. The idea is to experience another school system, get a fresh perspective on things and learn to be more autonomous. I'm not too eager to leave Ireland just yet but the prospect of being able to write an entire short story in peace, of having a whole room to myself and not having to queue makes me finally agree to set off for France.

I'm also profoundly relieved to stop eating maternal cheese for breakfast, lunch and dinner. It's been increasingly hard to draw the line between family eccentricity and insanity: the only reason our father doesn't serve us fried afterbirth burgers every day is that our mother only gives birth once a year and the highly nutritious placenta and vascular membrane dishes only last a day.

I get on with my French aunt and uncle rather well, not to say swimmingly, apart from a hitch or two at the start. The first source of conflict is that I expect my aunt to give me pocket money but it is never forthcoming. I wait for weeks and weeks and still no pocket money, so at last I write a letter to my mother to complain and the bone of contention is buried.

The other problem is triggered by the fact that without really realizing it, I begin to consume inordinate amounts of shampoo. Practically a bottle a week. I begin to wash my hair twice a day in an effort to look exceptionally clean as I've noticed French girls set great store by immaculately clean hair. Irish girls don't seem to care either way and usually make me feel entirely transparent. So I really pour on the shampoo and add on some of the stuff from my aunt's bottle of syrupy honey and chamomile conditioner for good measure.

I can scarcely help myself. The bubbly hair syrup pours into my hand by the bottleful. It must be emotional or monetary deprivation, possibly both. It feels so fulfilling to swathe the top of my head in the eggy amniotic mixture, to paste it into dollops of bubble-thickened impasto and smooth it down again into matted arabesques.

My beautifully-bearded uncle is the first to voice his objection. He summons his cavernous voice from deep inside his throat and cows me into using less household shampoo. He is right and I obey him as he is something of a holy hero to me. He comes down the stairs from Mount Sinai with his Biblical beard and God's wrathful message that the Golden shampoo calf is not to be milked.

To make up for his sternness, he buys me my own bottle of goop-green shampoo and tells me that it has to last as long as a month. I begin to dribble out shampoo in drops from that time onwards, slowly tilting the bottle like a pipette that carries a limited amount of ambrosia.

My third embarrassment is related in some strange symbolic way to the second one and perhaps also in an even more twisted way to the first.

Alone for the first time since my birth, I begin to give in to the potent signals my body has been sending. My attempts at wanking far from Ireland, however, are religiously plagued and remorseful so I promise the Supreme Being that I will stop miscreant masturbation. The promise is in the end impossible to keep and having started it so late in the day I find myself unable to stop. I begin to fear I've inherited my father's hypersexual condition and start to worry about overpopulating the planet.

Little do I know at the time that my system is being subjected to a redoubled onslaught of testosterone. My whole body is actually under the sway of chemical determinism. My penis is swollen with the DNA-altering substance, my heart hums with it all day and night, my testicles brim over chock-a-block with war-mongering, radioactive, fratricidal sperm. The potent natural steroid starts to hemorrhage out my pores and I am forced to resign myself to god-forsaken lubricity.

I don't actually know where I get the idea that God doesn't like wankers. I flick through the Bible over and over, but nowhere do I come across the passage that says "Thou shalt not idolize the genital apparatus." No one I know has ever told us that it is forbidden to immoderately partake of the Johnson. No Irish priest has ever preached explicitly against the perils of the penis, no teacher has taught me to resist the temptations of caressing the testes. And yet, there is a deeply-engrained sense of foreboding in me that penile polishing is a punishable offence.

Nevertheless, I finally justify the new-found hobby by deciding that if God had been totally averse to masturbation, He would have placed the penis between the shoulder blades, well out of reach. Of course, it dawns on me that the Tree of good and evil is also within Adam's reach, but I throw this objection to the back of my mind for the time being.

After having mastered the manual motions of straightforward masturbation, I therefore begin to enter the stage of experimental, fantasy-induced beating off. Just as my sixteenth year begins to loom, the dam-load of testosterone yields and is released into every recess of my body and brain. The substance bubbles and blossoms into a body-snatching plant. The dosage of the hormone coursing through my chemical-clogged, barely sperm-tight genitals feels colossal. I am suddenly compelled to wank a bare minimum of three times a day, sometimes in the most inordinate, uncomfortable risky places. I end up sailing very close to the wind.

Now that I have finally given in to temptation, my Johnson goes entirely berserk. It feels like a battle-enraged warping berserker Viking is thrashing it out in my underpants. I sense erections coming unbidden at all times of the day and spend the night nursing a penis so engorged and tumescent that it feels I have developed penile bone support. I must take after my father. This is my genetic inheritance. I fear I'm surpassing even Brian. The Priapic experience teaches empathy. For the first time in my life, I begin to gain compassion for poor sperm-filled Brian.

It's a relief that this Hulk-like mutation in my pants is occurring in my aunt's vast solitary mansion. So much space and no siblings. Thank God I can go through this phase without being encumbered by a queueful of jostling, jockeying, bickering, tiffing, pinching, biting, molesting, bothering brothers and sisters. I can only imagine what they would have called me (Olaf the Orgasm?) considering that Brian is afflicted with such an ignominious nickname for quietly relieving himself in bed and just a few times in the garden, despite the fact that we've established that he was actually just sleep-wanking.

As the months go by, my erogenous condition worsens considerably. I can think of practically nothing else and become what I can only call *polymorphously perverse*. Freud applies this term to infants, but it seems much more appropriate as a description of what I go through in my fateful sixteenth year.

I'm basically attracted to everyone and think about having sex with everything under the sky. And that's not being hyperbolic. I mean every possible thing. I even try masturbating with cutlery. I try attaching several baby spoons at a time, locking my mistreated member in a cold, steel embrace. I toss the turkey up against the bark of a tree, into a field of flowing wheat, onto a fresh drift of snow. I try screwing melons, watermelons, hollowed-out cucumbers and bananas, cloven kiwis, large tomatoes and a poor hapless apple.

When my foodophile drives abate, I try ploughing into eiderdown pillows, blankets made of wool. I ooze into silk, my aunt's watered fabric scarf (which is never quite the same again despite and also because of my panic-stricken attempts to wash and iron it out). My uncle's leather school bag, his wallet and three of his remote controls are violated and then cleaned.

I even try banging a drawer, a wardrobe, a shutter, a lighted lamp, a table, a chair and the sofa. I try quenching my quince against the window, the floor, moldy cellar walls, the dishwasher, the fridge. I would try choking Kojak against the ceiling if I could reach it.

In a word, to put it delicately, I engage in coitus with the whole family house, the sanctified villa my grandfather was born in, the place he so painstakingly bought back thirty years after his father was forced to sell, the place he reclaimed from collapse with hard-earned money and labor, the place he brushed up to a fine palatial finish with his own hands. But I have no thought for reverence and wank like there is no tomorrow, weeping sperm-tears by the tumbler, by the bottleful. I pour it out like syrup, ease it out like dollops of shampoo.

In Robert McLiam Wilson's *Eureka Street* - a novel I highly recommend - one of the characters shakes a chemical substance into his underpants making his Johnson look like a "nuked raspberry." I love the description, but it doesn't quite do justice to the look of my member at this point. My pecker is so bruised and battered it's beginning to look like a second-hand item on a low-brow Eastern-bloc flea-market, a bomb-damaged antique in an IRA firesale. The skin on my glans is as wrinkled and weather-beaten as Samuel Beckett's face on a particularly bad day.

My thoughts lead me to explore every avenue of pleasure. I fantasize about engaging in sexual commerce with all kinds of beings, even aliens, hybrids, animals and birds (running ostriches for the most part).

The only frontier I do not transgress is polishing the banister in public. I remain and ever will be an intensely private person despite the fact that I'm now telling you all this.

My newly found habit only starts to be a real embarrassment the day I am heard beating off in the toilet.

After frenetically flogging my frog for close to half an hour, I am finally getting close to summoning the tadpoles, when suddenly I hear an angry, throat-clearing sound, repeated at intervals, from the other side of the toilet door. It becomes impossible to concentrate knowing that someone is listening, so eventually I wrap up my penis and step outside the door, trying to look as carefree as I can.

But my Aunt is there in front of me in the corridor, looking about as joyful as the Grim Reaper. Stock still, she is waiting, nodding her head slowly, biding her time, casting a cold eye on life, death and me. She is giving me the most reprehensive stare I have ever received, and takes her time subjecting me to every nuance of her disapproval. Then she asks me in an icy clenched voice what I think I am doing.

I manage to keep down too great a blush and bumble that I am just coming out of the toilet. She stares me down and hisses in a loud vicious whisper

"You know what I MEAN!"

And that is the end of it in appearance. She never mentions it again.

But my French aunt - more puritanical than any Irishwoman I know - has got me filed away for good in her terrible bad book of boyish perversions. I can hardly blame her really although I feel unfairly browbeaten. From that moment onward, my aunt's pussy begins to rank very low on my ramshackle roger's Richter scale. She continues to treat me with a crescendo of suspicion, a rapid decrescendo of affection.

Girls of my age are still the main target of my cuffing, but gaining access to them is no easy achievement. I am far too shy to do more than flirt semi-skillfully and the closest I come to kissing a girl on the mouth is a bit of a tooth-knocking disaster, despite the fact that there is nothing more sexually available than a hot-blooded Southern French teenager teeming with Mediterranean-heated hormones.

In one of the schools I stay at in Cannes, I even encounter a girl called Chloé who tells me at the lunch break while we're sharing an egg and ham sandwich that she is deeply ashamed of being a virgin at fourteen. Chewing her half of the sandwich, she looks at me with beseeching, bewitching blue-green eyes and an imploring pulpy red mouth.

Chloé is gorgeous by any standards and a young male in his right mind would diligently deliver her forthwith from the humiliations of virginal bondage, but for some reason I can't really fathom, I fail to rise to the occasion.

Is it the recent emergence of AIDS-related paranoia? Am I the first guy she has come to with this reasonable request? Is it that I'm afraid that she will prove too French and hot to handle for my inexperienced greenhorn fingers, with my virginal Irish snake still safely vacuum packed in my pants? Or am I just too rootedly romantic, despite all my home experiments, to accept such a bare offer of free loveless lust?

Whatever the reason, when I finally fall in love, it is not with Chloé but with Paola. She is my Italian first cousin from Milan and also my age. She is a witty, enchantingly quixotic queenlet with impish, dark brown fire in her irises, and a mouth fashioned to make a thousand men leap in the sea.

Above all else, the smell of her hair is pure intoxication. Strange to say, it's not exactly what you might call a pleasant smell, in any conventional sense. I mean, it doesn't smell of fruit shampoo or cinnamon and honey. And yet it is the potion that tips me over the side of the boat.

To put it bluntly, it is actually a smell of greasy hair that clings to her head like a halo - even after a shower. When our families go off camping on a Swedish island, she doesn't wash it for over four days and then it really reeks to high heaven, placing me in seventh heaven, cloud nine. Without even trying, she has lashed me to her soul and made me pine for nothing but hair grease. I find myself caught in the web of her hair by the glue of her sebum.

Although the experience is ultimately painful, at last I learn something that many people will never understand in our odor-suppressing culture: love is a greasy, blissfully smelly thing, and over-washing and deodorant nips the true stuff in the bud. Don't forget that, poor brainwashed reader, you know it in your heart.

Both my soul and semen are willing participants this time, but I find that after much flirting and flitting and holding my hand, despite my passionate show of interest in all things that regard her, she simply does not fall in love.

Does she see me as family and therefore off bounds, in a sexless cousin category? Am I too young for her, not handsome enough, insufficiently Latinate, over-Celtic, too low on feral hair pheromones? Too eager and intense? Not greased enough myself? Too happy-go-lucky, too lackadaisical, too low-comedy, too madcap? A combination of all these?

Despite my shortcomings, Paola lets me kiss lips and eyes. I perform these gestures in a state of religious awe, inhaling the fragrant fumes of her sebaceous secretions like incense.

She even lets me squeeze and caress her infinitely firm, bountifully bobbing bubble-breasts. But for some reason which haunts and defeats me, she is unable or unwilling to let herself slide into the sea of love with me and my trustworthy semen.

Unaccountably, she gives the impression of liking me and continues to smile and laugh into my face with her gorgeously open mouth but will not succumb, despite all my overtures, serenades and ministrations.

Then she has to go back to Italy and I am left to sip gall in Gaul. The next time I see her is for Easter. It is cold in Milan and she is keeping me at a firm arm's length, pretending I'm not even there. Her attitude has changed entirely. Is it the temperature? The recent entombment of Jesus or the tampering of time?

Even her brother seems distant, laughs far less at my jokes. The stubble of manhood is beginning to appear on his cheeks. He is becoming as ursine as his father and seems to have outgrown me. I'm a no longer funny amusement that has fallen out of fashion.

When the family goes out to *la chiesa* on Sunday, I stay in their home and do something I would never have done before.

I go into Paola's room, rummage through her things and try to understand why she won't be my girl. In a corner, behind her bed, I find a drawing that I gave her. She hasn't thrown it out which is something, but it doesn't exactly have pride of place on the wall above her bed.

I look into her drawers and find a pair of knickers to cherish, a string of brownish rosary beads, a pair of color-striped socks to nuzzle and inhale.

I find her diary and shuffle through it to those summer days when she would take me by the hand and whisper secrets in my ear, but there's nothing. No mention of any feeling whatsoever. The most I find are the words *Vacazione con i cugini.*

I flick through the autumn weeks, reach Christmas, the Italian celebration of Epiphany, and there, at the end of January, is the dagger icicle that stabs me straight through the chest. In large blaring capitals, surrounded by heart shapes, smiles and exclamation marks, I read the horrible words that stay with me forever:

PAOLO, TI AMO

I put back the diary in its place and turn from the room in despair.

But in the end, of course, she does not marry Paolo, she marries Vittorio nine years later. There is some conflict, some marital boredom, so I'm told. I greet this news with cold but thankful comfort, sucking a wolf's tooth like a lozenge on my tongue.

In my mind, she is mine, mine forever at the age of sweetness. I can go back to her whenever I wish and feel the bubbles of her laughter burst delicately on my face, kiss the nub of her navel, plough the fold of her vagina, with its dark nether sun-burst of pussy fondant.

I finger the flesh and the holes in her soul, breathe the air of her hair. Paolo and Vittorio are watching us in stupor at the door of her bedroom. There is nothing they can do.

The Cold War continues when talks between Reagan and Gorbachev break down. Lake Nyos in Cameroon suddenly releases a cloud of gas killing nearly 2000 people. An earthquake strikes San Salvador killing 1500.

Desmond Tutu becomes the first black Anglican bishop in South Africa. *The Phantom of the Opera* opens in London. The centennial of the Statue of Liberty is celebrated in New York harbor. *The Simpsons* is created.

17

Sartorius

Ronald Reagan undergoes prostate surgery. U2 releases *The Joshua Tree*. An eighteen-year-old West German pilot evades Soviet defence systems and lands a Cessna plane on the Red Square in Moscow. I return to Cork in an Aer Lingus 747.

After a year on the Continent, I am now back in Ireland in the family madhouse with my multitudinous, multifarious, mayhem-loving siblings and my disturbingly eccentric parents. This being said, now that I have gained some perspective and seen a few Parisian art museums, I realize that our parents fall short of being full-blown surrealists. Although we continue to be subjected to placenta burgers and maternal cheese, milk, yoghurt and lollies, it isn't as if our mother is Leonora Carrington getting up at night to snip a lock of hair from the sleeping heads of unsuspecting guests, mixing the abducted filaments with eggs to make hair omelettes for breakfast.

Neither is our father quite as bizarre as Max Ernst or Salvador Dalí, despite the fact that he is very fond of imitating the Spanish painter, twining an imaginary wisp of a moustache, rolling his eyes and drawling in heavily accented Spanish:

"The only difference between me and a madman is that I am not mad!"

We don't exactly have to bear the embarrassment of our parents walking a full-sized ant-eater on a leash through the streets of southern Ireland, but at times it does feel a bit like that.

At an age when fashion, or at least the importance of being presentable, is beginning to impinge on my sense of what is allowable or wearable in public, our parents still take us on long evening walks, dressed invariably in clothes that have not been renewed for decades.

The most embarrassing detail to us is not the threadbare flares they flaunt when everyone else's legs are encased in skin-tight jeans, or even the flowery, neon-bright shirts our mother favours when everyone else in the island of Ireland considers grey a gay color. It is the woollen hats they both inevitably sport once the sun has set. And atop each hat, at the tip of a length of tapering wool, a fluffy, snowball pompon wobbling in the wind.

We brace ourselves and cringe as neighbors approach and our father booms out his inevitably convivial, old-fashioned Frenchman's greeting. The Irish men and women on our block are invariably courteous, usually managing to quash their amusement to the corners of their smiles as we discreetly beat down burning embarrassment, tempering the shame into shields.

As I have said, Martin Montcocq's mind is still in the midst of the Second World War and everything that can be must be repaired or regenerated in the name of the war effort. He will spend the rest of his life using and preserving things until they can no longer hold together. And even then there is always adhesive tape, glue, thread or wire.

Martin wears the rips in his clothes like war-torn medals, the bullet-holes of Time. If a streak of dirt manages to add itself around a moth hole or a rent in the fabric, then that is all the better. Martin Montcocq even begins to fancy our mother for the first time the day he sees her rushing to a lecture as a student on the campus with a stripe of bicycle oil on her calf.

Shoes are key items in our parents' dress sense. Anne wears the same three pairs for thirty odd years. Martin wears his late father-in-law's shoes even though they are at least two sizes too small for him.

Both of our parents regularly rummage through bins every weekend. Separately or together, they rake through junkyards to scavenge. If we're not asked to participate, we generally stand by, impassibly registering cries of parental glee when a rainworthy coat is found, a pair of trousers that fit, a sock that can be matched with an almost similar one lying at home. We have a massive chest of drawers that contains literally dozens of second-hand hats, gloves and scarves. You hear of celebrity singers having a different pair of shoes for every day of the year. We have a somewhat less glamorous version of that.

So if our father can be construed as Surrealism's enthusiastic poor relation, a kind of Salvational Dalí, or Max in Earnest, our mother is Leonora Carry-a-ton.

You might think that with such sartorial confusion at home, it's a relief to go to school, with its orderly, mandatory uniform, the compulsory, standardized tie, the regulated clean shirt with its homogenously, impeccably cut blazer and feint-ruled pants; bizarrely enough, it's at school that I personally experience the most sartorial estrangement.

Although we are school-raised in the only co-educational establishment in the city, which mercifully allows some interaction with the opposite sex outside of siblings, diversity is not encouraged at all. Girls wear the same uniform as boys (with just a nondescript grey skirt to indicate genital belonging). A number of vigilante teachers train hawk eyes on every detail that diverges from the official color code. A tie that deviates from the authorized burgundy can draw a screech from the menacing machine who teaches us math; a sock that's too light a grey can trigger an unending diatribe against the perils of sartorial depravity. Occasionally, a pupil goes so far as to venture white, on pain of death.

With all the open-mindedness and liberal thinking infused in me by my parents, the idea of appearing in plainclothes one day never occurs to me even in fantasy, although I have numerous nightmares. Brian also confides that he dreams of walking barefoot to class in our father's overlarge pyjamas.

Of course, the theory behind the uniform is well known: it is meant to inspire a sense of respect for authority, orderly conduct, it is designed to limit social discrepancies, erase a sense of teenage individualism. There is even a potentially spiritual message behind the uniform as it is supposed to promote anti-materialist habits and indeed in our school there are no Giorgio Armani blazers, no Dolce & Gabbana T-shirts. Nor does anyone bother in those days with Cardin underwear, as far as I know.

And yet, despite all the regulation, the whole scheme is a shambles. Hidden, toilet violence is rife amongst pupils; weak or boring teachers are ragged and hectored without mercy; money is worshipped almost as much as in Monte Carlo and social distinctions are abundantly visible through the wear and tear of unrenewed uniforms. Perhaps the only feature that it fosters is the eradication of originality. Difference is successfully viewed by all and sundry with a suspicion verging on disgust.

The compulsory place we have to inhabit in order to receive an education takes on a decidedly alarming cast for me when a large number of pupils start to develop a kind of para-uniform, a set of outer clothing which incomprehensibly manages to escape the censor's tongue-lash.

This parallel uniform presents itself in the form of a greatcoat, known to initiates as the parka, an indispensable item for the cool Irish teen crowd, the official members of the Inner Party. And around the feet of the parka-wearer, grows a tar-black excrescence, what I see as a manure of molten lava, a thick-soled, ankle-covering, dark-laced boot that swallows the calf like a boa.

Although the white sock is considered to be beyond the pale of the permissible, unfathomably the parka and double club foot boots never fail to pass muster. And the worst of it all is the fact that these boots seem to be modelled on those worn by soldiers of the Waffen SS.

Almost unbelievably, the khaki-colored parka carries a small German flag stitched to the shoulder. It's beginning to look as if the disbanded legions of the German army are reconstituting themselves in the ranks of Irish youth. Why of all flags, the German?

I learn in history class that despite the Irish government's putatively neutral line during the Second World War, it tended to favour the Allies. Only the IRA briefly consorted with the Nazis in the hope of overthrowing Britain. Despite this apparently undisputable fact, I begin to see my classmates' dress sense as the expression of Ireland's subconscious fascination for Nazi Germany, growing like a second skin over officially sanctioned uniforms.

Of course, there is nothing as dramatic as Fascism going on, and Irish (and British) secondary schools are really very gentle versions of the concentration camp. No deaths occur, at least not in my school camp, just mildly unbearable bullying, the gentle prodding of the stick in your heart. Mind control in our school is no more than a tightly-strung band to mould the shape of your skull, a finger stirring your brain.

But even these memories are but the Expressionistic after-images of a childhood that is really rather happy. Ireland, which I still prefer to call Sartorius when referring to my teenage years, is by no means an entirely dystopian location, and when I finally reach university I can hardly believe that the secondary school camps I have been through exist in the same country.

Iraqi war planes drop mustard-gas bombs on Iranian residential areas. Palestinian cartoonist Naji Salim al-Ali is shot down in London. 11 people are killed by the Provisional IRA at a Remembrance Day service at Enniskillen. Typhoon Nina kills 1036 in the Philippines. Starbucks Coffee begins to spread across America. Ellen Page and Evan Rachel Wood are born. Rita Hayworth, Andy Warhol, Erskine Caldwell, James Baldwin and Fred Astaire die in their separate ways.

18

The Perils of Comfort

The cargo ship Khian Sea deposits 4000 tons of toxic waste in Haiti. Perestroika begins. The Supreme Court sides with Hustler Magazine. The Eritrean War of Independence rages on. The first McDonald's opens in a country led by a Communist party in Yugoslavia. The Soviet Army begins to withdraw from Afghanistan. 100,000 people sing protest songs in Estonia during The Singing Revolution.

Despite my inevitable difference as the offspring of an eccentric Francophone and a somewhat alternative extreme Catholic feminist, despite the fact that in Sartorius I tend to be seen as a Frog or a Faggot (both qualifiers not quite hitting the mark), I do have friends at school and even girlfriends, or at least one steady one who, with some measure of culture shock, manages to date me for over a year.

Sartorius is in its seventh rainy season when I meet her. Enough rain spits down from the Catholic sky to submerge the city. The floods in the greens and street corners are there for so long the suburban dwellers in my vicinity begin to view them as ponds.

I walk her home through the squelching, soggy paddy fields, thanking the rain for inconveniencing our steps into making our hips and shoulders knock together. We wade through an endless football field of mud to get to her place, dribbling the ball of desire, weaving it round our feet as we step round the muddier patches, for ages not daring to score.

Connie's father is the main hindrance to that as he regularly barges into his daughter's room whenever we are in there alone, treating us to a glare or a rough, abrasive word. He is really quite a charming man, once you get him going on his favourite subject which is invariably potatoes, Sartorian music and the most eminent national novelist. He is rather cultivated despite the fact that he has never received much education. With time, he even comes to enjoy my presence, especially after he discovers I can be lectured to (having received ample experience with this in my father's company).

Before the sudden decline in our relationship, he takes to giving me an avuncular tap on the back, gives me a record or two, preparing coffee on more than one occasion. He even begins to counsel me in the fine art of handling women, advice which I secretly deride, having recently read D. H. Lawrence.

One day, he places a hand on my shoulder. With the tone of a man who has drunk deep from the pond of knowledge and swallowed its salmon, he says

"You know, we men are sometimes better off leaving de Missus alone..."

Long, meaningful silence ensues. I stare into his motionless eyes, trying to grasp his intention. When he sees he has made me sufficiently uncomfortable, he dives to the depths of this insight:

"It sometimes means you have to push your own need to the side ... if you get what I'm after. I'll put it this way, maybe we're better off watching the Telly or reading the Paper and leaving her be by herself..."

I nod in silence, but then decide to add that maybe women need us to make them want us. As I venture this, all I can think of is Connie sheltering a chick in her hands, nestling it between her breasts.

He looks at me as if I have just talked of a parallel world, a place that has nothing to do with Sartorius. His eyes take on a lost look for an instant, but he snaps out of it and looks at me with a smirk of derision.

"I do it myself," he counters, "sometimes, I just sit down on de sofa, watch de news or a filum, and de woman is better off without it."

I let it go at that and we remain on congenial terms for another few months, until the incident for which he never forgives me.

His daughter makes it clear that intercourse is out of the question. Reciprocal, interlocking genital friction is fine as long as it doesn't lead to what she refers to as "sex", saying the word as if it is a deeply engrained kind of insult, something filthy and dangerous like putting muck in a wound.

"My Da would kill me if he tought we were having it", is the reason she gives. The leaf-flecked, light-catching amber of her irises glint solemnly.

Her father sees me as a harmless Frenchie with his Frenchie ways, but submissive. Not the type to do the dirt or soil her maidenhood. Until one day, he finds a book I have given her for her seventeenth birthday, hidden under the mattress.

Alex Comfort's *The Joy of Sex* is still all the rage in Britain and America. It has finally found its snaky way onto the shelves of bookstores in Sartorius.

When I come back a few weeks later, giving him time to appease the bolts of his anger, he stares me stonily in the eyes. I am given to understand that I am to be "Tolerated but no longer Welcome."

From that time onwards, he avoids being in my presence. When compelled to do so, he stays on endlessly in the same room, usually the kitchen, our only refuge, as the bedroom and sitting room are now way off limits.

On one occasion, he comes in to clean the sink with a sponge. I can tell you, I have never seen anyone clean a sink so thoroughly: he washes and scrubs and rinses and bathes and scours and rinses again a countless number of times, a real labour of love, the tongue of the sponge licking every recess, every cranny, every shiny surface.

Then he stares down into the shaft of the sink as if he is looking down a well, for endless minutes, trying to catch sight of his reflection at the bottom.

The only time he speaks to me in that glacial period of Sartorian history is to deliver a somewhat threatening anecdote. His wife, Mrs Sweeney, who is a professional knitter of Aran sweaters, has agreed to make one for me, having been asked by my mother who in turn has agreed, against her better judgment, to get me a brand-new jumper for my birthday, conceding to this extravagant request only because Aran knitwear is known to last more than a lifetime.

One day, as Connie's father is gazing at his wife knitting the patterned wool into her lap, seemingly lost in thought, he says

"Do you know that every traditional Aran jumper has a different pattern on it?"

I am delighted that we are now on speaking terms again.

"Tis true", he adds, "and d'ya know why?"

Three German soldiers pass in front of the window.

Mr Sweeney pauses to look out at them and then leans his beaky nose in my direction. Looking me directly in the eye now for the first time in four months, he says

"It's because people need to be able to identify fishermen who have drowned."

He stares at me hard, and then walks out of the room.

I take it as the threat it is, despite Connie's remonstrations that he is just trying to act the hard man. I am given abundant confirmation of this menace each time I wear the jumper.

"It's-a-lovely-Aran-sweater-you-have-there", he comments as if the sentence is actually one word. A sharp slit of a smile briefly animates the stone-dead features of his face.

And yet, with all those veiled and not so veiled threats, I do not end up face down in a flooded paddy field with only a stitching of wool to identify my waterlogged remains.

Connie and I break up some time later because she feels too young to take it further. Much later I learn with some surprise that her parents have also split up, and stranger still, that her father has seemingly disappeared into thin air.

Living as a lodger down in the outskirts of the suburb, near the woods, his clothes are found one day in a pile, sloughed like a moult at the foot of a giant elm tree. No trace of him is ever found again.

Nelson Mandela celebrates his 70th birthday in prison. Nasa scientists testify to the Senate that man-made global warming has begun. Thousands of protesters are massacred in Burma during the 8888 Uprising. Al-Qaeda is formed by Osama Bin Laden. The Iran-Iraq war ends leaving a million bodies behind. A cyclone in Bangladesh leaves 5 million homeless. Adele, Rihanna, Conchita Wurst and Emma Stone are born. John Carradine, Jean-Michel Basquiat and Ella Raines cash in their chips.

19

I Get into College and then a Vagina

Ronald Reagan says goodbye to the nation. Barbara Harris becomes the first female Episcopalian bishop. Iran places a three-million-dollar bounty on Salman Rushdie's head for writing *The Satanic Verses*. The Estonian flag is raised again. Georgian protesters are massacred by the Red Army. More than a million protesters march through Beijing. The first crack in the Iron Curtain occurs: Hungary takes down 240 kilometres of barbed wire from its border with Austria.

It is the year of my eighteenth birthday, the year of the Leaving Certificate. I have to get into University and the (mostly self-inflicted) pressure is high. I am about to leave Sartorius to enter the Kingdom of Higher Education.

You don't need that many points to get into what I want to do but I take this final secondary school exam as a test of my worth. Brian is no threat but I don't want to look shabby next to Deirdre and Sif who have already skipped a year because they're so bright.

Entry to the Kingdom of Higher Education, otherwise known as University College Cork, depends on the number of points you are able to get with each grade. An A is worth 5 points, a B is 4 points, a C is 3.

To get into Arts, the Humanities, you need a mere 16 points. To enter the Beta category of Law School requires 25. It takes 29 points to get into the Alpha category of Medical School, and an unbelievable 31 to become a vet.

I decide to skip the classes I feel I can dispense with at school, working with more efficiency on my own, but this selectivity brings down the wrath of those teachers whose classes I miss. As a result, I'm labelled as the school's No. 1 black sheep until I desist and for another two or three months after my surrender.

Despite playing truant, or perhaps because of it, I miraculously manage to squeeze out 27 points in the final exams, which is enough to get me into both Arts and Law. Deirdre and Sif of course get 31 and 30 respectively which allows them both into Alpha Medicine. With some prodding on my part the following year, Brian attains an honourable 20 and is able to follow his older brother into Arts.

The ambient philosophy in Ireland at this time (and probably in most countries) is that if you can get into something prestigious then you should do it regardless of whether it interests you or if you have an affinity or genuine aptitude for the subject. So, for the most part, people only do Arts because they haven't been able to get into something that requires higher points.

Thankfully, I manage to dunk Beta prestige and financial reward for interest. Our father congratulates me on being "the recipient of an independent mind."

But with the hectic preparation for these final exams and the absence of any possible girlfriend, I begin to lose the first marbles of my mind.

It happens gradually, as these things do, and at first, I don't really notice it. To begin with, it's just small things like spending a whole afternoon with fuzzy tunnel vision (which, according to Deirdre, Sif and Siobhan, is the defining feature of maleness anyway).

It's mostly just a shimmering fluctuation at the centre of the eye. On other days, I have the vague impression that the world is a checkerboard and I start avoiding the cracks in the slabs of the footpath.

On some days, I am so intoxicated with study that I become a black knight in leather armour to slay Dragon Math, to subdue the snake of Irish Literature. Studying over much does strange things to my brain. My sisters say I'm becoming a hermit. Even Deirdre gets out more than I do. Sif and Una claim I must be schizophrenic.

Brian is ignoring me. He says I never listen to what he says, which admittedly is more than partly true. I admit I find it hard to concentrate on anything that isn't a book.

Just after the exams, when the tension hasn't yet begun to ease off, I start to experience OCDs accompanied by a strong strain of male hypochondria. I know nothing about obsessive compulsive disorders and refuse to really acknowledge that I have them.

It all begins with things like a morbid fear of death, danger at every corner. I fear my heart is going to stop any second, my lungs are going to stick together and refuse to unstick. An imaginary cancer develops in my left testicle which suddenly seems bigger and harder than the other one.

I'm also afflicted with a kind of aggravated Keats Complex, fearing that I will meet his fate, knowing that I will never have his talent even if I live to a ripe old age but attempting to produce poems that rot before the ink is out of the pen.

After having had my soul badly dented by my break-up with Connie, this girl-less period leaves me feeling brittle and homeless. I begin to go for walks around the green in front of our house holding a cup of tea in my hand and mumbling to myself. I wonder if I'm ever going to have another girlfriend, if I'll ever be able to experience feelings for someone else.

It's on one of these midnight walks that I have my first hallucination. I still don't know if what I see is a spot of incipient schizophrenia, the distractions of a lovelorn mind, or an Aisling (a female allegorical representation of Ireland).

What I see one fateful evening is an entirely naked woman whose skin is a velvety purple. No crone figure at all. She's actually a little like an International Klein Blue version of the Lollypop Lady who used to help me as a child to cross the road. I can't believe that the Lollypop Lady is naked in front of me, slowly, casually, making her way through the trees.

What's also a little surprising is that the Lollypop Lady seems totally unconcerned by her nakedness. When she turns to look at me, she smiles and puts a finger to her lips to silence me even though I am not about to say anything.

She looks searchingly into my eyes, takes a deep breath and says something I'm not really expecting, especially since I have never really been interested in politics.

"Vote for Mary Robinson, and your soul will be saved. A little Mariolatry goes a very long way."

I nod my head mutely and then unstick my lips to hoarse-whisper

"I was going to anyway."

When I enter college in September, the summer has had its healing effect. I have had a failed fling which goes as far as kissing a French girl whose lips are so chapped my head feels like a detachable gourd being positioned on the mouth of a girl who has crossed a desert and is on the point of croaking her last breath. Nonetheless, I begin to recover and feel that I still hold some appeal.

After a month of college back in Cork, I meet an Erasmus student in a bar. She is drinking a snowball, a fluorescent yellow cocktail I have never heard of. Her name is Dominique Lacourgette and she offers a lot of eye-candy in her unbuttoned shirt.

Dominique is actually pretty gorgeous when smiling, despite the fact that she smokes. When she stops smiling though she puts on a disconcerting attempt at sex appeal which has the unfortunate side effect of making me feel somewhat queasy. The sex appeal stare makes her look like a genetic cross between Lauren Bacall and a deeply unhappy bulldog.

I try to keep her smiling throughout the conversation.

Although all things considered I don't really find her a turn on, I can sense that Dominique is the kind to have sex with a stranger and I feel very much like a stranger at the moment. And I've never had sex.

I walk her home through the darkening streets, past the sweet shop of my first primary school days, past the school where I first experienced the epiphanic splendor of Ruth Kelly's bottom.

Dominique stops me by a black, wrought-iron gate, gives me her most fervent canine stare and engages my mouth in a kiss.

I have never kissed a smoker before. As most people who have tried it will know, it's like being tongued in the mouth by an ashtray.

I unstick my lips from the saliva-sodden ashtray. Dominique looks up at me and treats me to a bit of Bulldog Bacall.

I hurry Dominique down to her bedsit, worried in case I will change my mind and leave her there and go home with my virginity intact. I'm so desperate for something to happen, I'll do anything.

By the way, gentle reader, if you don't care for unwholesome, graphic, risky, risqué, un-PC descriptions of intercourse, don't hesitate to skip to the end of this chapter. What I'm about to describe deserves to win The Literary Review prize for the worst depiction of sex.

It may also irritate you if you feel that female characters should always be rendered in a conventionally dignified, ideal light. If you have a distaste for naked bodies (both male and female), it is also advisable to avoid perusing the paragraphs below. In fact, if you find yourself in any of these categories, you should really put down the book. There is inevitably going to be an increasing amount of sexually explicit matter as I enter my late teens and early twenties. Throw the book in the fire or give it to someone you dislike.

Before I have quite got past the doorway to her bedroom, Dominique grabs me by the arm, pushes me down onto the bed, and strips me like a doll down to my underwear. Bending over me like a nurse, she injects the full slug of her tongue into my ear making my whole head feel like a shell receiving the assault of a snail in a hurry to get home.

Then Dominique begins to mouth my eyes, nose, mouth and chin, lavishing what feels like liters of saliva.

She even sucks on my protuberant and hairy Adam's apple as if it's the tastiest ice cream in town.

When my entire headpiece is completely moist and glistening, she begins to drag her amazingly prehensile taste organ down the rest of my body, literally licking off my underpants. When my penis suddenly springs out, bobbing buoyantly, Dominique issues what sounds faintly like a bark.

The blowjob she bestows is somewhat voracious, suppliant and surreal, making my dick feel like a rubber dog bone. Despite being deeply grateful for her unbelievably generous efforts, however, I can only describe the sensation as barely more pleasurable than having one's genitals encased in a formaldehyde solution during a Britart experiment.

Nevertheless, I now finally know what fellatio is, and feel profoundly honoured to be taken with such succor and solace into someone else's mouth.

But then Dominique does something far more surprising and pleasuring, something no woman will spontaneously, in all likelihood, ever do to me again.

She unclasps her Scheherazade shock of hair, letting it fan out over her shoulders in dark wispy flames.

With a flick of the neck, she casts the whole swathe of hair like a net over my nakedness.

Drawing herself down like a human-shaped brush, Dominique drags her cotton-covered breasts over my skin and in their wake every filament of her hair, letting the mass of her mane pour down the length of my body, from the crown of my head to my cock, to my toes, repeating this capillary shower until parts of me are tingling and other parts twitching.

Dominique releases me gradually from the exquisite torture of her cat-o'-nine-hundred-tails, and watches me writhe in the aftermath. When the sensation subsides, she graciously bends over, puts her long-lidded, smiling Bacallian eyes to my flesh and butterfly-flutters her lashes over my steadily melting virginity.

But suddenly, before I know it, I find myself yanked up from the bed like an inanimate doll again, leaving me standing half-unconscious. Besotted with sensation, I can just about make out that Dominique is taking off her clothes.

She lies down stark naked on the bed.

I tell myself that she is expecting similar treatment or at least the activity known as cunnilingus, but instead she does something that sends tremors through the core of my Irishness.

Before my disbelieving eyes, she pulls her feet upwards with her hands, forces her legs back to what seems like breaking point and manages to position both of her ankles right behind her neck, telling me bluntly to stick my member into what she designates in French as her "wet mussel."

Let me pause this picture for a few paragraphs the way they do it in contemporary films, freezing the frame while the narrator-hero tells you his feelings or comments on the action.

At this moment in my college education, I am reverently ingesting words like "objectification", "male gaze", "negative stereotyping" and all the other concepts that underpin feminist theory.

What is an ardent young feminist like myself to make of the young woman before me? Something in the situation fails to tally with the orthodox precepts of the theory I am learning with Professor Cox in English 3.2.

Is it wrong to look upon the pussy of another with such unabashed boldness? Is not this French woman offering herself up to the gaze? Are not these thoughts of mine examples of objectification? Is not this very pause in the narrative a breach of feminist etiquette?

Reader, do not misconstrue my intentions. Why do I sense that you feel I am forcing you to stare at Dominique's proffered pussy? Please do not think that I am trying to rub your nose and your eyes in Dominique's moistened labia. Above all, I am asking you to consider the bewilderment of an eighteen-year-old virginal male literature student who has gone from experiencing modestly clothed friction in the Irish dark to witnessing more than full frontal — indeed, oysterous — nudity in the dazzling French light of a bald bedsitter lightbulb.

My knowledge of vaginas at this point is limited, to say the least, but Dominique's vagina seems to me alarmingly exquisite. I am certain that by any standards and in all objectivity, Dominique is endowed with a fine-featured, delicately-rimmed flesh jewel.

Nevertheless, as I'm sure you can understand if you have gone on to read this, I'm a little taken aback by the suddenness of the young Frenchwoman's request, not to mention the strangeness of her newly forged body shape. My hard-on is starting to wane under the shock and the pressure of having to perform and I'm also somewhat turned off by what to me at this point in my Irish boyhood looks increasingly like a mussel-shaped alien beckoning mutely on the bed.

If Dominique could read my thoughts, I would no doubt be out on my ear and I can sense Professor Cox's disapproval of me too. All I can

The Pleasures of Queueing

think of now is a multitude of Academic voices lecturing on theory.

So, what do I do?

Being a novice, I tense up all the muscles of my body, mistakenly hoping that if my body is braced it will give me penile support, like a stake on a plant.

I manage to keep most of me erect but somehow fail to shove the essential semi-flaccid part into the officially sanctioned place. Dominique's oyster seems to harbor a whole array of clitoral pearls, multiple entries, sliding jellied portals, slithery side-doors, smooth slippery slopes outlined in abrasive urchin hair and a multitude of walled-up windows, or is it just the one or two that keep recurring?

When I finally get the tip of my glans into what appears to be roughly the right place, it wiggles out, thrashing and flopping like a boneless baby seal. We don't have a condom and the fear of AIDS is now also dogging my spirits, alongside Professor Cox and the unideal reader.

What happens in the end?

Dominique gets me to relax a little by getting on top (thanks be to God for resourceful women), but my demoralised dick is so bruised, battered and numbed by the grating of thick pubic sandpaper (both my own and hers) that I don't feel a thing.

The whole affair is so unarousing that Dominique's poor harassed vagina begins to go dry and then it feels like I'm thrusting weary Willy into the abrasive armpit of a hemp-covered hair-shirt.

She asks me to go to the bathroom to get lubricant and I gratefully, painfully comply. But when I get to the communal bathroom at the end of the hall, I find myself in the same situation as when my mother or sisters ask me to retrieve a needle from the bathroom haystack of bottles, boxes, pots, cases, containers, tubes that the average woman's cosmetic paraphernalia inevitably entails. I never find the exact product they're looking for.

There is no lubricant in sight in Dominique's forest of medicines, lotions, shampoos, liquid soaps, eye-liners, nail-polish pots, mascara vials, tissues, pumice stones, hair brushes, nail clippers, hair driers, cotton pads, cotton buds, tampons, panty liners, Body Shop substances, and the usual jungle of unidentifiable objects.

The closest I can find to a lubricant is an old tube of foot cream, caked at the top with an unsavoury yellow crust. And it's a good two years past the sell-by date.

In resignation, I press out a hardened swab of the foot stuff and smear it over my weather-beaten, crestfallen, purple soldier.

When I get back to the room, after much concerted effort, we finally get my bald-headed yoghurt slinger to come to liquid effusion. I should say it's actually more of an insensate muscular spasm.

The whole thing is ultimately a mechanical, soulless affair with no palpable pleasure or affection on either side. I go home delighted to have done it.

*

In July, I decide to head out alone for the first time. It's the age of the InterRail pass, a limitless train ticket that allows young travellers to travel through Europe for a month in any direction they like, with limitless mileage. In other words, you can chug it up and down from southern Greece to the Arctic Circle in northern Norway every two days if you feel like it and have the stamina. And it's pretty much what I attempt in the first spurt of enthusiasm, until I realize that even a young person has a physical endurance limit.

Because I go off with not much in my pocket, I avoid paying for accommodation and use the train as a hotel. If I go past my daily budget, I take a train at around midnight, sleep sitting up, lying on the seats or the floor. If my destination takes only four hours, I go past it, get off the train at around three in the morning and get another train back to the place I want to visit. The craziness and freedom of this is exhilarating. I go island-hopping in Greece under 43 degrees Celsius, hot-train it up to Lillehammer in Norway, see my first and last blue glacier in the middle of summer, sleep in a field of heather and cloudberries, cross the Arctic Circle and the wilderness.

The Pleasures of Queueing

Students unveil the Goddess of Democracy statue in Tiananmen Square. British police arrest 250 protesters for celebrating the Summer solstice at Stonehenge. A 600km human chain is formed across the three Baltic States in a bid to claim independence. Food riots occur in Argentina.

The Guildford Four are released after 14 years. The communist governments of East Germany and Czechoslovakia resign. The Romanian Revolution begins. Daphne du Maurier, Lawrence Olivier, Salvador Dali and Ayatollah Khomeini all kick the bucket.

20

Wallflowers

Thousands of people storm the Stasi headquarters to get a look at their files. Margaret Thatcher resigns after eleven years in office. The first McDonald's opens its doors in Moscow. Nelson Mandela is released. Germany is reunified. The Baltic States and Namibia declare independence. Mikhail Gorbachev is elected. Food poisoning kills 450 invited guests at an engagement party in Uttar Pradesh. *Misery* and *Wild at Heart* are in the cinemas.

Dominique finishes her Erasmus year in Cork and we decide to remain friends. I go to see her in Paris for Christmas but it doesn't go well. She argues persuasively that I'm not really in love with her. It is pointless to go on. As well as this, she has met another Frenchman who is great at anal sex. The anus, she adds in an equivalent idiomatic French expression, is an entirely different kettle of fish.

I reply that despite my lack of experience, I too could surely be proficient, given a little practice, in the probably not-so-complex art of anal intercourse.

She answers that it is she who does the sodomizing.

When I laugh a little in astonishment, she gives me a hefty slap on the face. She has been longing to do that for a long time. We nevertheless part on good terms when I go back to Ireland.

Surprisingly, it is out of this slightly humiliating, fruitless trip to Paris that the first proper stirrings of a desire to write a novel emerge. Although I am still very young to write autobiographical fiction, I have too little knowledge of others to write about anything other than my family, and the experience of inhabiting the Montcocq household is like being dropped every day into a large human ant-pile.

The snag is that writing a novel, even a domestic post-war memoir such as this, in the midst of the Montcocq menagerie, is no carefree blissful enterprise. When I settle down to write at the desk that I share with Sif, Deirdre, Brian and Thorsten, Sif barges in to inform me that I am using the desk on her time-share, even though she's not availing of it. She and Deirdre are sticklers about shift space. She has to do her homework she says and the desk is not under my jurisdiction at this moment of the day. So I trundle my enterprise off to Ian, Una, Emil, Samuel and Aine's desk but get pushed out after ten minutes for trespassing.

I check in the other twins' rooms but there is someone sitting at the desks in each room. The sitting room table is occupied by another eight of my siblings, the kitchen table is crowded with Siofra and Siobhan's homemade pastry experiments and the toilet seat is exuding the unwelcoming smell of at least half a dozen recently unloaded bottoms.

I try sitting on the ground but within minutes my back starts to ache and my right leg goes numb, so I amble aimlessly around the house for a while with my writing paper in my hand and resign myself to standing in the queue by the sitting room door.

After half an hour of listening to Colm and Grainne quarrelling and jostling over the merits of using cardamom in Danish pastry or mixing peanut butter with cloudberry, it is finally my turn to sit at the table.

The problem with trying to write in the living room is that it's a far cry from writing in the city-centre library. To put it euphemistically, the quality of the silence isn't exactly top-notch. When there isn't a sibling or two or three crawling under the table in search of trouble and adventure, routinely tickling, scratching, pulling, biting or licking legs that get in their way, that's a propitious start. The ceaseless soughing of whispered conversations or homework discussions on either side of you is enough to distract a sadhu from the depths of meditation.

And then there are also the interminable questions of younger siblings importunately asking you to spell the word "beautiful", the word "forehead", "thorough", "lieutenant", "paean" or "onomatopoeia".

In between these questions, in moments when the steady breeze of whispering abates, you attempt to concentrate, you try to focus on the still blank page lying spotlessly empty on the table in front of you. You finally begin to write a few sentences and then you stare into space, looking for the right word and/or inspiration. You wonder where the Muse is hiding, and then your Mother comes in.

It's potentially very risky to be seen staring at the wall by your mother. Your mother cannot abide indolence, and gazing at the wall with a blank page in front of you is tantamount to wasting your time. If you really have nothing to do, or feel like daydreaming or moseying around, the best thing to do is to hide. Lock yourself up in the toilet or find a nook or a cranny where you won't be spotted.

If your mother catches anyone alone and palely loitering, she will find something for you to do. And that something is something you will not want at all. You will be given one of your mother's countless, unimaginably boring tasks to accomplish. Your mother's chores are not the average drudgery of unloading the dish-washer or hanging out the clothes. No, she will ask you to do things that could be done more quickly than it takes to explain what she wants.

Here's a typical example. You are called to the kitchen from wherever you are in the house and asked to fetch something that is practically already within reach of her hand, deep in one of the nearby cupboards (you will not be told precisely which cupboard as this is something that you are expected to intuit from the tone of your mother's voice).

If you're particularly unlucky, you will also be required to root out an object the nature of which has not clearly been specified. For instance, you can be asked to look for something like a sponge, but she won't necessarily use the word "sponge" to describe what she wants. Sometimes, you will hand your mother the right object, but it won't be the right color, the right shape, the proper utensil she requires for the particular task with which she is employed. If you protest at being abused in this way or claim that you're pressed for time, you will be called a self-centred brat or some similar term of endearment.

So, when my mother comes in this time, her authoritative belly bloated to its maximum capacity with another set of twins, I quickly put pen to paper and write the first thing that comes into my head. I write something that has nothing to do with what I intended, which is arguably one of the defining features of creative writing anyway. And the upshot is that the sentence is actually not entirely bad. It has a certain spontaneity and indirection that actually inspires me to write a second sentence and a third, almost oblivious now to mother's roving eyes. It's amazing how constraints can actually bear fruit.

Another force I have to contend with, however, is one I mentioned earlier. My old friend and lifelong companion, Attention Deficit Disorder, the cognitive impairment I acquired from too much dandling and involuntary head-butting in infancy. In recent years, I've learned to come close to harnessing the more exasperating manifestations of lapsing concentration, enough to prepare for and pass exams, but if I don't concentrate on the act of concentrating, my mind wanders virtually uncontrollably.

ADD does not just mean that you have trouble focusing on the conversation you may be engaged in because you've got something else on your mind. It means that you can't even concentrate on the thing that's on your mind. It's a bit like listening to a radio with a freely rolling tuning button. The broadcast is set on politics in the Middle East but before you know it you're also vaguely listening to *The Eye of the Tiger* mixed in with snippets of Simon and Garfunkel's *Bridge Over Troubled Water*, the middle of which segues into an Albinoni adagio crossed with Beethoven's Fifth-Ninth-Third symphony and a Irish talk show about bullying in schools, and then you're back again to the news about Irish nurses picketing outside Wilton Shopping Centre and how that doesn't fit in with the end of the Soviet Union and the bomb planted by the IRA.

So you see writing, or even attempting to write a novel, when you have that level of exterior and interior disturbance, is a feat in itself, no matter how poor the novel, no matter how disjointed the style, no matter how aimless the plot, how paper-thin the characters, no matter how drifting the focal point. There should really be a literary prize for the best novel ever written by a writer afflicted with ADD who has radios broadcasting from every room in the house, every area of the brain, an exponential, incremental number of siblings, a hawk-watchful mother, and an increasingly eccentric and money-stinting father. The winner would be Olaf Søren Montcocq. Hands down. Every year.

I think about the acknowledged writers who have had to contend with adverse conditions and (subjectively speaking) none seems as bad as mine. I mean ok there is Alexander Issajewitsch Solschenizyn who had to write his novels in a gulag in Siberia with vicious guards, frozen fingers and nothing in his stomach and I agree he should definitely be eligible for a special prize just for that. I can only begin to imagine writing under Soviet duress with your fingers barely able to unlock from frostbite.

And yes, of course, there is Arthur Koestler who should get an official accolade as the only writer to have written a novel under torture. I mean he practically wrote *Darkness at Noon* on the rack with his head under water and his feet in the fire.

The list of afflicted, woebegone writers is long, and each deserves mention and laurels. The World War I poets wrote sonnets to the stink of the trenches and mustard gas and the non-iambic beat of the bombs. Knut Hamsun wrote *Hunger* without having eaten for weeks (I wouldn't be able to write a sentence without having breakfast). James Dickey had to write *Deliverance* at night to keep his soul alive after his day at the office. The Irish writer Christy Brown managed to write *My Left Foot* with his own eponymous left foot and nothing else to help him. Afflicted with locked-in syndrome, the French journalist Jean-Dominique Bauby dictated his novel *The Diving Bell and the Butterfly* with his left eyelid. Richard Ford was able to become a first-rate stylist despite his dyslexia. Philip K. Dick wrote some of the most challenging science fiction novels ever conceived in spite of paranoid schizophrenia and drug addiction. Both Iris Murdoch and Terry Pratchett wrote their last novels in Alzheimer's arms. Peter Redgrove wrote his final poetry collections in the grip of Parkinson's and a number of other crippling afflictions. Les Murray is a recurring nominee for the Nobel Prize despite Asberger autism.

The list of contingencies and infirmities goes on. And yet, there are times when the level of disturbance, the degree of intrusion and persecution in this house makes me envy John Bunyan writing happily in his cell, almost asking to be thrown into prison by the pro-Catholic hegemony, almost begging to be taken away from his wife and kids to be able to write in the peace and quiet of his cell.

"Olaf, what are you doing? You're lookin' so sareious."

"I'm trying to write a novel."

"Aren't you supposed to be doin' yar homework? Dis is da homewark table."

"I don't have any homework. I'm in college now. I do assignments. Essays. You have two months to do them, so I do them when I feel like it."

"Don't ya feel like itt now?"

"No, I don't actually. I'm trying to write a novel. Two novels."

"Why'r ya writing two hovels?"

"Novels."

"Yeah, why are you writing two hovels?"

"That's actually a good question. I don't really know. I shouldn't be doing it. It's just that I've had two inspiring novel ideas and I don't want either of them to go stale so I've started both at the same time. It's probably because of my ADD too. I keep thinking about one idea and then the next. So far, anyway, I've managed to keep the two ideas developing separately, in two separate copy books."

"Couldn't you put da two togedder? Dass called a subplott. We learnt datt wid Miss Glynn. In King Lare, like, you have datt. Two plots. Glynn says de subplott is actually stronger dan de main plot in dat wan. She says iss not a good ting."

"I've thought of that, alright, but I can't find a way for the two novels to stick together. I mean they aren't even in the same genre."

"Whatt're dey bout?"

"Yeah, Oluf, tell us da stories!"

"Ok, well, the first one is actually partially inspired by life in this house. I've called that novel *My Family's Sex Life and Other Oysters*."

"Ur family's sex life? Jesus, Olaf, Mum'll kill ya when she finds dat out. You better not have dem put it in de shops!"

"*Putain! Elle va te tuer!*"

"Shut up, Thor, Dad can't even hear ya. He's gone ta see Didier."

"Okay, don't worry about it. I probably won't get it published anyway. I'm mostly just writing it for practice. I'm trying to get better at writing, see, and the only way, I've been told, is to write as much as I can, which isn't exactly easy with you guys around, talking and horse-playing all the time."

"Jesus, Olf, yar such a bloody snob! You'd tink you'd sprung outta Jupiter's tie."

"Did ya write about de twins? Der having sex I'm sure of itt. Dare gointa kill ya if ya write about dem."

"Look, I've changed all the names anyway, so don't piss me off, ok! It probably won't even get published."

"Watt does published mean? Like, put in a pub, is it?"

"Oh, God. Deirdre, will you just tell her? Put her out of her misery. I'm tired of this conversation. I need to get back to my work."

"You haven't told us bout de second hovel! Wass datt wan aboutt?"

"Yeah, tell us what ya put in yer nostril!"

"Ok, quickly then. The second novel - not *hovel* or *nostril* - is a science fiction story. It's what you call a speculative novel, which means it's set in the future but it's about the present as well. My present really."

"Are dey boat about you?"

"Jaysus, Oluf, yar so vain. Can't ya write aboutt sometin differen?"

"Aoife, just, fuck off, ok? I didn't ask for your opinion."

"Oh, dare he goes again. Mr High and Mighty witt de upper class accent. Are ya trying to copy de British? You'd swear you were a Brit sometimes, de way you go on. Can't you talk normal Cork English? I'm tellin ya. Yar like a fuckin Beefeater. And a poster of Diana on his wall!"

"Shut up, Una, let him speak and tell us da story!"

"Ok, just quickly then. I want at least half an hour of silence after that. Understand? Perfect Silence. Do we have a Deal?"

"Yeah, ok, Olaf. Half an hour. We gotcha. We'll go an' have a cuppa while yar doing yar wry tin."

"Ok, well, this one is set in the near-future. A post-apocalyptic world.

Actually, they've had a Third World War but about thirty years ago and society is starting to pick itself up again. I've set it in Canada. Anyway, there's a city which is trying to foster the arts again so it organizes a writing competition in which the candidates have to try to write a novel at the top of a skyscraper in an area of the city that's been deserted. Parts of it have been bombed, but not by dirty nukes with fallout. The area has several uninhabited skyscrapers that have just been left standing. They're old and dilapidated, but relatively intact. So, anyway, there are ten finalists, each writing at the top of a separate skyscraper. And I'm one of them - I mean my hero is one of them. The competitors are dropped off by helicopter and they have enough food and drink to last them half a year. They're given a chemical toilet placed on a corner of the skyscraper, a tent, a sleeping bag, some extra clothes, a pillow, a chair, a writing desk, twenty pens and five reams of paper in case they need rough work."

"Do dey have ta use the writing paper for da toilet?"

"No, they have proper toilet paper too. As much as they need. It's loaded onto the skyscraper by helicopter at the start of the ordeal in sealed plastic wrapping to protect it from the rain. I thought it would be too autobiographical to leave out proper toilet paper, and a little bit implausible."

"Cool enough story. Tell us de rest."

"I haven't thought it out yet."

"Ah, go on Oluf! You've got us hooked now, fuck sake!"

"Well, I've just started, so I don't really know how it's going to end yet. It's just an idea, really. I'm still just writing bits and pieces of it, not in the right order. The young writers on the skyscrapers start writing and you get extracts from the books that they're writing directly transcribed in the overall narrative. It's a study on how place impacts the nature of what you write."

"Is it abow nature?"

"Olf, will you show us da book when iss finished?"

"Fuckit, doan tell us! Dare are zombies in de buildings!"

"No, Aidan, there are no zombies in my novel."

"Would you read de hovel to us for bedtime?!"

"I suppose I could, but I'm not sure I could read all of it to some of you little fellas and girls. Some of the subject matter is a bit - grown-up, if you see what I mean?'

"Why doantcha put a few zombies in wan of da buildings?"

"Grown-up? We know all about grown-ups, for Crysake, Olaf. We watch dem on telly. We see dem in school. We have two at home, and Deirdre, Sif and you are as tall as dem. Sure even Brian de Sp-. Brian is as tall and fat as Mum."

"You could have Superman too. He could knock out de zombies! Why don't you have Superman in yer nostril?"

"Well, ok, I'll see about reading it to you. If I ever get it written! Now off you go to the kitchen. Go have a cup, and be back in half an hour to finish your homework. Go on, scram! Go and talk about zombies!"

"Deirdre, can I go for a poo?"

"How many times have I told you that going to the toilet is an inalienable human right? You don't have to ask me."

*

After having completed the three first chapters of each of my noise-fuelled novels, I misguidedly manage to get back together with Connie for a while. Her father has flown the coop, disappearing up his tree like the legendary crow that King Sweeney became. Now that paternal shackles have dropped, Connie is ready to have sex, but hangs her head in deep disappointment when she finds out I have recently lost my virginity. Still, she is eager to be relieved of hers now that she's come of age and quite a few of her friends have been able to get rid of theirs.

I am of course willing to relieve her. I am still very much attached to Connie, despite the fact that she has been unfaithful to me twice.

We agree to meet in the thick of the night in early April when the cold is beginning to ease up. Her house as a venue is still out of the question since her mother is, though not quite as churchy as Connie's flown away father, a stickler in matters of the cunt and the cock.

The other problem is my parents' house is now as populated as a doss house, so any privacy is unlikely to be attained, even in the toilet. So finally, Connie and I agree to have sex in the caravan now mouldering at the back of our junk garden.

The sheets of the caravan berths are musty from having spent the winter without heating and the cold makes them rough and unwelcoming.

I nevertheless manage to exude a certain confidence, unfurling a condom with the ease of a seasoned cigarette roller. Connie lies on the sheet, her eyes staring wildly at my genitals and the ceiling of the caravan as if my penis is a pistol about to release violent white bullets into her unprepared vagina.

We warm up a little under the hard sheets and the mouldering blankets and everything is going relatively well until I begin the insertion procedure. Rearing to burrow, I position my gorged and congested, heat-and-humidity-seeking mole, in roughly the place I think it should be on the starting block. But the expected penile foothold is nowhere to be found. For some unfathomable reason, I am again incapable of locating the entrance. This just seems to be a completely different vagina. How different can they be? I realize with mounting anxiety that my experience with Dominique hasn't prepared me for virgins and yet I now have to prove that I have acquired the know-how.

I have never understood why some men have a relish for virgins. If you're in any way sensitive to other people's pain, deflowering a virgin is a guilt-inducing, frustrating, dispiriting experience. Having to inflict pain in a state of arousal is about as morally uplifting as poking your finger over and over into someone's wound while they helplessly lie back and pretend to like it.

And I haven't even mentioned the penis that after twenty minutes of fruitless endeavor feels about as wanted as a Polish immigrant in post-Brexit Britain.

In his Calvinist elitism, God has made location of and access to vaginas for beginners a heart-rending enterprise, like trying to assemble a furniture kit with apparently missing holes, the wrong kind of screwdriver and diagrams that don't explain all the steps. You know what the finished arrangement is supposed to look like, but you haven't a clue how to get there.

Finally, it takes another good few fumbling, slip-sliding attempts to correctly insert my flopping flesh-screw into what is the correct, IKEA-approved, somewhat overly small slot. It's a good thing my purple-headed DIY handy-man isn't claustrophobic.

It doesn't help my concentration or confidence (and I won't even mention erotic joy) that at this stage in the confusion Connie is starting to look like a silent movie version of Shelley Duvall in *Shining* when Jack Nicholson tries to break into the bathroom with his axe.

When everything is finally in the right place and locomotion has started, I make it as brief and painless as possible, moving slowly without bucking. Within minutes the condom is full to the brim with the milk of human kinkiness and I withdraw, mistakenly thinking that Connie will be grateful that the event has been brief.

I walk her home through the night across the silent roads of Cork, past the Church of the Really Cool Presence, past the cow-shed architecture of Bishopstown Community School, down into the mellow lamppost lights of Melbourne Road. Little do I know that it is to be the first and last time we make love.

When two weeks later I suggest that we try having sex again, she says bluntly "I don't think I'll be wanting it all the time" and I am left to consider the spatio-temporal gap that separates the French world of Dominique Lacourgette from the Irish world of Connie Sweeney.

My mother tells me that in matters of heaven and the heart, patience is the cardinal virtue, but Connie decides once again that we are on a break. I tell her that in the context of our bond, "break" is something I cannot accept. The word "break" is fine in the context of Kitkat bars or school recess but a break in a relationship is next to inconceivable. She says nothing and then it is over forever for the second and last time.

I immediately go into mourning, am found writhing in pain, literally on the floor of my room. I reel with intimate hurt like none I will hopefully ever feel again. My sisters bend down around me in various positions of compassion like in paintings of Christ being taken down from the cross to be mourned by the Marys. They comfort me with tissues to wipe my eyes and my nose, one Mary holding my head in her

The Pleasures of Queueing

arms, another cradling my legs, another placing a solacing hand over the spear-wound in my side.

For the second time, despite the comfort afforded to me by my ministering angels, I begin to feel another splinter of pathology wedge itself in my brain.

Aoife, Deirdre and Sif go out to buy our favourite apple pie, the one that comes in the silvery tinfoil platter and is sprinkled with visible sugar. Siobhan, Aine and Frieda go down to prepare tea. Grainne, Una and tiny Anna stay by my side, cooing, saying soothing things, taking it in turns to tickle my sides when it looks like I'm about to cry.

For the first time, I feel truly blessed to have so many siblings, so many little ministering mothers. When our parents come home from their Saturday shopping spree, I am dry-eyed and smiling. We are all busily accumulating dollars and real estate on the Monopoly board that the little ones have insisted on playing.

*

In early June, as soon as I finish my exams, I start off again on my own on an InterRail pass, heading straight for Germany this time as all the exciting news has been happening over there since November. I want a piece of the action, a piece of the Wall.

The so-called *Mauerspechte*, Wall Peckers, have been pecking away at the concrete, unofficially demolishing the border between East and West, pulling it apart, nibbling at the holes in the endless long grey biscuit of hard, concrete politics.

When my train pulls into Berlin Hauptbahnhof, the air is electric. There is singing and shouting and screeching in the streets, the Reichstag is covered in graffiti. People are drinking, shattering bottles against the buildings. There is debris all around. In the parks of the *Mitte*, people are sunbathing and picnicking half-naked or naked, running around in Elysium. It feels like Paris must have felt to my father in 1968.

I make my way up to Invalidenstrasse, and there, suddenly, stands what remains of the Wall. It is crumbling, pock-marked and perforated with all manner of holes. But it's still dauntingly there, barring access to the street. I follow it up Kieler Strasse, then take a right into Boyenstrasse, past the Kirchhof Dorotheenstadt II into Gartenstrasse, and then I'm in legendary Bernauer Street where the underground tunnels were dug down through cellars and floorboards by defectors fleeing *homo lupus sovieticus*.

The green grass in front of it is covered in rubble, tourists and drunkards, bicycles and backpacks. My plan is to sleep in Friedhof Sophiengemeinde, the nearby graveyard which I hope won't be overcrowded with the living.

Little do I know that I am about to commit the most inglorious act in my existence, something I will remember with more than a shiver of shame.

When night falls at last around ten, most of the tourists leave. The noise level begins to diminish. Drunkards are asleep or have wandered off to other parts. I skirt around the graveyard and find shelter behind a group of moss-covered gravestones, rolling out the thermodynamic Swedish sleeping bag that my father has bought me. I slip it over my body and fall asleep shortly after to the far-away sounds of singing and celebrating.

When I awake in the middle of the night, I am surrounded by a group of about twenty young yobs.

I sit up and stare, heart hammering in my head, trying to catch my breath and get a grip on the fact that this terrifying moment is actually happening.

One of the youths, a skinhead with an angry-looking rash of tattoos spreading from his arms to his neck and right up over his left cheek to his forehead, is beginning to rummage through my rucksack as if I'm not there.

Two multiply-pierced punks begin kissing in front of me, with much ostentatious wrestling of tongues.

"You vant to trink vit ass?"

The man who has addressed me has stubble on his chin. He looks older than the others and appears to be the leader of the group. I'm not sure what he's asking me. The meaning begins to clarify when he rips the top of a beer bottle off with his teeth, thrusting the bottle onto my chest.

"I ... um ... actually, thanks, but I don't really drink."

Terrible answer.

The Pleasures of Queueing

Stubble-face looks me straight in the eye without smiling this time. He prods the beer bottle roughly against my lips.

"You trink, ok, *mein Freund*. Dis iss free Berlin, you have trink now, wit ass, or I fuck you. *Verstehst Du? Dieser blöde Kerl ist komisch, was denkst Du, Heinrich?*"

"Don't vorry. Wolfgang is only fucking vit you. He's not dat bad. Trink de beer and natting vill happen."

I take the beer in my hand and they all go silent as if watching something that really has pizzazz. At least I know the beer hasn't been spiked or tampered with. It was opened in front of me.

I sip at it a little, still looking wary I suppose, and they all burst out laughing.

"*Gott*, iss dat all you can do? Why have you come here, if fun you are not going to have? Listen, if you trink de whole bottle in van trink, vee promise not to fack you."

I drink down half the bottle and they send up a raucous cheer, clink their bottles and knock hips.

"De whole bottle now you moss finish... Good, now vee some gut vodka trink, yes. What dink you ann dat?"

Oh, gentle reader. Need I go on? The evening, as you have no doubt surmised by now, ends in what can only be called pure debauchery. I am embarrassed to put it down in words, and yet our less habitual acts define us to some extent at least. So, if you are to have an accurate picture of who I am, or at least what I have experienced, I need to tell you what I do that night in some detail.

It is not so much that I enjoy a regressive passage for its own sake (although why not after all) but I feel that if you are to have a proper, fully-rounded understanding of a character, you must see him depicted in an act that holds no real relish of salvation, at least not in the eyes of a good Catholic boy like myself.

So, to go back to that unholy night, here I am, starting to totter under the effect of beer, vodka, then plonk. We wallow out of the Sophien-Gemeinde cemetery onto Bernauer Strasse, take a collective leak against the Wall, wander past Kirchhof Strasse Elizabeth, if I recall properly, roll around in the grass a bit, get up again, try not to get knocked down on Brunnen Strasse, get a little lost in the side streets and end up again on Bernauer Strasse where the *Mauerspechte* have pecked holes in every part of the Wall.

This is where Wolfgang stops us, saying we are now to play a game. Manhandled into submission, I am requested to strip off my clothes along with all the others and line up in a queue about twenty feet from the Wall, one woman, one man, in that order. I end up sandwiched between a naked young woman in front of me and a naked man behind me. We are then asked to close our eyes until Wolfgang gets things organized.

It's a game he calls "Political Pecker."

So we line up in a queue, a little nervous but laughing, with our eyes more or less shut while Wolfgang makes seven girls and three guys follow him through a hole that leads to the other side of the Wall. We hear him shouting from behind to make sure we keep our eyes shut, but I think I've more or less guessed what's about to happen and Hans is gleefully spilling the beans on a game they've visibly played several times.

"Hans, shut de vuck up! It's supposed to be a zurprise. Make sure dat the eyes of Olav our guest are gombleedly glosed!"

The young woman in front of me in the queue is called Hannah. She turns round to present herself, depositing large Teutonic breasts on my chest. She is at least as drunk as I am and splutters in my face. Her cupid-bow lips are more than a little appealing and the shower of sputter is surprisingly exciting. I lick off the sputum and look down to find my penis at half-mast. We both laugh at that and Hannah bends over and takes my organ in her fist, handling it roughly like a rock star with a microphone. She croons on the glans, then pretends to be a newsreader announcing the Berlin broadcast in English.

The guy behind me is Herbert and he keeps shoving his genitals up against my buttocks when my back is turned. I have to admit it's not entirely unpleasant, but as an Irishman I have been reared to beware of all enterprises that require a second penis.

Nevertheless, although there's something decidedly inglorious and unglamorous about this scene, I begin to perceive the full potential of queueing for the first time in my life. As a species, we tend to see queueing as an irritating waste of time, a bit like an extra-carceral death row of boredom, when in fact it could be a great source of pleasure, a chance to make new acquaintances, to rub off people that you might otherwise never come up against. Queues are great social levellers, potential breakers of barriers between sexes, age groups, ethnicities and classes. They allow you to come into proximity with all kinds of people with captivating pheromones.

Apparently, only 2% of married couples meet their spouses in a public place. I'm sure the human race would be a whole lot happier if people met their life partners in queues rather than at work. If you think about it, the workplace is somewhere you end up for the most part because you make the wrong vocational choice (or don't have much genuine choice to begin with), so meeting someone there is really like compounding errors.

If you meet someone in a cinema queue, there's a good chance that you will have a pleasure-based hobby in common. A definitely good start. Meeting in a queue for the Eucharist at church is a match made in heaven, and you're already in front of the altar. If you make yourself meet your partner in an art exhibition toilet queue, you can look forward to a lifetime of art loving and lesbianism. We should really start queueing clubs in which everyone queues just for the sake of queueing in a spirit of total interaction.

As I think of this solution to human solitude, my eyes are shut. An ocean of blue grass and alcohol is swirling in my head.

When I open my eyes to see what's going on, the smaller holes in the Wall have been filled with what looks like naked human buttocks, both male and female, though it's sometimes hard to say which is which. It's distinctly surreal. Flowers of flesh embedded in the Wall.

"Ok! Each *Mann* into his flower! Ve are going to play Vall Pecker! Dose who remain in de queue, vatch und learn! Hansel, are you ready? Let's get started!"

Hansel, Friedrich and Lenz run towards the wall, bounding like beige rabbits in a midsummer night's dream. When they arrive at the Wall there's a bit of fumbling, but after arousal and insertion they each start to pound the wall flowers with their hips. I am left watching the spectacle, my head spinning, not really certain that this is actually happening.

After moaning to a stop, Hansel and Lenz withdraw staggering from the Wall.

From behind the Wall, I hear "Next!"

I close my eyes again to slow the spinning in my head.

When I open them again, Hannah in front of me has disappeared.

A moment later, the voice behind the Wall shouts "Next! Olav! Olav! It's your turn to play!"

I wobble uncertainly towards the giggling flesh bricks surreally stuffed in the daunting grey slab of the Wall. The slit in the middle is glistening with seed. I hesitate for a moment, but Wolfgang's braying voice eggs me on to fire my sperm into one of the two that are already doused.

For some reason, I hesitate, and before I can make up my mind to head over to where I think Hannah is, the hole in which she has inserted her buttocks is already being foraged by Herbert.

I get down on my knees to manoeuvre my loins in front of the only bottom that's left, and before I know it, my wallpecker is in and I'm blindly, rhythmically, thumping a flower and the Berlin Wall with my thighs. I really don't feel anything except an overall slipperiness in the cool grey slab of cement. The alcohol in my blood has numbed me and all I can think of is what Wolfgang is shouting. We are fucking the Wall! We are sowing the seeds for a better tomorrow.

When I wake up late in the morning, all of them have gone, even Hannah. I wander back to the cemetery to gather up my belongings, head straight for a hospital, get an AIDS test and a hotel for the night.

The US and Russia agree to end the production of chemical weapons and destroy most of their existing stockpiles. Czechoslovakia holds its first free election in over 40 years. A stampede in a pedestrian tunnel leading to Mecca kills 1426 people.

Leonard Bernstein conducts his final concert. Women's suffrage is authorized in the last Swiss canton. The channel tunnel links Britain to mainland Europe for the first time in over 8000 years. *Dances with Wolves* and *Total Recall* are released. Ava Gardner, Greta Garbo and Roald Dahl meet their maker.

21

Ars Amatoria

After almost 50 years, the Cold War comes to an end, and the Gulf Wars begin. The Soviet Union dissolves into 15 sovereign republics. America establishes its outposts in the Middle East. The Provisional IRA launches a mortar attack on 10 Downing Street. Bombs explode at Paddington and Victoria Stations.

President Bush declares victory on Iraq. He is hospitalized briefly for irregular heartbeat. Mount Unzen erupts. The Angolan and Ethiopian civil wars begin. Spacelab is carried into orbit. Boris Yeltsin becomes president of Russia.

In traditional marriage plot novels, there are typically two or three suitors vying for the heroine's heart and hand. Each claimant stands in contrast to the other two, embodying a way of life, a profession or an attitude. In the following chapters, our hapless anti-hero (me) encounters two further women to whom he initially fantasizes about pledging troth when, as Jane Austen puts it in her great novel *Emma*, "the train with all its carriages of plush chairs and chinaware went rumbling down the mountain, derailing brutally into the shimmering waters of Shit Creek."

This is the year in which I meet Fiona. She's a girl who seems like the perfect synthesis of Connie and Dominique in that she is a beautiful young red-headed Irish woman with freckles and yet not prudish in the least.

As Oscar Wilde once put it so perceptively, there are two tragedies in life: one is not getting what you want; the other is getting it.

On the positive side, Fiona modifies my conception of what it is to be Irish. In fact, she almost completely annihilates my preconceived notions of essential Irishness.

I meet her in an amphitheatre in an Eng Lit class on *Frankenstein*, in which the Professor is discussing Mary Shelley's *homme fatal*. I am still a bit depressed but keen to pierce the mysteries of Literature and as entranced as I can be in my dejection by what the lecturer is telling us concerning the genesis of the novel - how the inexperienced Mary Shelley had a nightmare that inspired her to write a better, more interesting story than her poet-lover Percy Bysshe Shelley and Lord Byron himself.

I have a particular fondness for the Frankenstein myth, having been Olafstein as a toddler due to the recurrent head wounds I sustained and being an assemblage of eccentrically mismatched cultural fragments.

We are being told that *Frankenstein* was inspired by Luigi Galvani's experiments in what came to be known as galvanism: he and his followers were apparently able to make dead frogs and even the corpses of human criminals twitch and move their limbs when enough electricity was channelled through their bodies.

It is at this point in the lecture that I feel a curious, slightly electrifying sensation crawl up the lower part of my calf. I look down to find a shoeless foot nudging its way up and down my trouser leg, slowly, almost thoughtfully, like a foot that is daydreaming or rubbing itself into sleep.

I look up to find that the owner of the foot looks entirely disconnected from what her foot is doing to the distracted, over-excited hairs on my leg.

The young woman next to me is graced with delightfully subtle features, especially those dreamy, slightly globular eyes. She is listening to the lecture in rapt attention and seems totally oblivious to both me and the doings of her foot.

I am scared to move lest she remove her foot or realize that she is not rubbing it against the seat in front but against a very human, male, sentient calf. I am paralysed with pleasure and very reluctant to relinquish these illicit moments of luxury.

Are these not the best erotic instants? When a stranger presses the entire mass of her voluminous breasts against your arm or your chest as she brushes by you in a tightly-packed bus, when you come up face to face, almost mouth to mouth with a knock-out beauty as you turn a corner and she seems in no hurry to get away but you are worried that she will think you are trying to harass her in some way so you quickly dodge out of her path and walk on feeling both elated and downcast at the same time.

The foot suddenly pauses, moving away. I am utterly dismayed at the idea that its owner has realized that she is not rubbing the bag in front of her or the edge of a seat but the leg of a young man on the verge of capillary overdrive. The hairs on both of my legs are all fully erect, branching outwards like antennae as far as they can possibly stretch.

But then the foot is back again, this time with more insistence. The toes become playful, almost wilful, as if they are practising toe scales on a piano.

I look up at the foot owner's face, almost fainting with arousal. She is still staring straight ahead of her, but this time there's a smile lurking in the corners of her lips and the more I stare, the more the smile broadens.

She draws back her head a little with a slightly haughty stare as if to say 'do you realize how lucky you are to be enjoying my foot with impunity?' I return a hot and bothered stare but remain gazing directly into the eyes of the she-elf. To lower my eyes now would be to lose her on the spot. So I keep on gazing at this girl who with her sensually-tilted head makes me think of Renaissance depictions of Judith after she has successfully severed Holofernes's head. The one by Cristofano Allori in the Louvre, most especially.

Why this attraction for the femme fatale I cannot help but wondering, as my mind tunes into Professor Cox's voice. Are men really such masochists? Our course on feminist theory at the University has instructed us that male painters and writers indulge in this kind of fantasy as a way of expressing their misogynistic fear and/or hatred of women, but that seems like a simplification. Surely the exact opposite can also be claimed. Are not these artists expressing their deep longing and fascination for powerful, self-reliant women who are so desirably strong that they make them lose their heads?

I neither fear nor hate women, on the contrary, and my fascination for depictions of Judith, Salome and Medea is triggered, I think, more by a willingness to be ravished, to relinquish the role of the dominant male whose hand-me-down duty it is to make all the moves if the relationship is to go anywhere, especially in Ireland. Who ever said that all men enjoy being a head taller than their partner? Who ever said that all men like to feel that their partners have weaker muscles and can be pinned effortlessly to the bed?

We stare at each other for what seems like five full minutes and the young woman resumes rubbing my leg, this time with a look of knowing audacity. When the lecture comes to an end, we remain seated and she asks me my name.

After a nervous gulp, I manage to murmur "Holofernes."

She nods her head slowly, and smiles.

"My name is Fiona", she whispers, "but you can call me Judith if you like."

There is nothing more alluring than a self-possessed, knowledgeable, intuitive woman.

We decide to go and take a cup of coffee at the campus bar. Parting after three hours, Fiona makes me promise I will show her my poems and novel extracts and our next meeting is set for three evenings later. I go home and start a short story about an expatriate office worker who becomes a toucherist and spends his free time rubbing up against non-consenting people in packed Parisian metros.

A week after that, we are already experimenting with do-it-yourself sex toys. Fiona has confessed a liking for what she calls ithyphallic sex. This, she explains, involves having various objects placed in her vagina while a partner stands aside and watches her savor them.

The first weekend, she undresses to reveal a bottom so curvaceous and smooth I feel I could canter five times round the paddock. She bends over on all fours and I watch her slip a pasty peeled egg deep into the precious folds of her pussy purse. She tells me she is moving it up to the edge of her uterus and down. When what she calls her "yoni egg" is on the verge of popping out, she draws it slowly back inside. By the time she is finished explaining and illustrating the workings of the yoni egg, the pressure in my pants is dam-splitting.

There is nothing obscene about this artistic performance. In fact it would be obscene to use the word obscene to describe what is really the most beautiful thing I have ever seen. This placing of yogic yoni eggs between Fiona's glistening lips is more absorbing and mesmerizing than viewing the Grand Canyon, the Taj Mahal, the Machu Pichu in one sitting.

Fiona's exploits favor the cosmopolitan. She tries inserting a Spanish cucumber, an Irish carrot, a Brazilian banana, a German sausage, courgettes from Cameroon, a Peruvian potato.

I would not be surprised to find that you feel this is all in poor taste, that even if it did happen, you're not supposed to write about such matters explicitly. The good thing about a novel though is that, unless the art department of the publisher's imprint has chosen a showy, naughty cover, you can read these bawdy bits in public without attracting unwanted attention. If you peruse a porn magazine on the bus - I have tried it and don't recommend it, especially not if you plan on time-travelling back to 1980s Ireland as you do it - you will get nothing but hard stares from the pious folk or from the ones who feel that the woman on the front cover is going to give little children nightmares in which they are pursued by naked ladies trying to smother them with their breasts. It's a well-known fact in Ireland and most countries around the world that a naked woman is far more dangerous to look at than a fully-clothed gangster with a gun.

Ok, perhaps I have given your imagination enough to fuel itself through those long winter nights, but perhaps I have not. I'm sure there are some of you who are thinking "A Peruvian potato? In a vagina? Are we really expected to believe that a high-flying, militantly feminist Anglo-Irish literature student would contemplate doing such a thing? Does Peru even export potatoes? Does it even have any? Would a potato not be too clumpy and round? Would a mud-caked potato not irritate the poor mucous membranes of Fiona's vagina? What is going through Fiona's mind as she shuttles these vegetables in and out between her legs with the well-heeled muscles of her richly innervated fibromuscular tract? Where, if anywhere, is this factional memoir even going?"

Let us take it that you have had enough. As for those readers who would like more than physiological hyperrealism, I must admit I have no idea what is going on in Fiona's mind, or even my own mind come to think of it.

Enough digressing. Let us resume the story of what it is like to encounter Fiona at this point in my life and how she permanently modifies my conception of what an Irish woman can be.

If I recall rightly, I was mentioning how forthright she is at the beginning of our relationship.

The second point I want to make is that in 1991, although Fiona is clearly a staunch, serious-minded feminist, she is still very frisky. By frisky I mean feisty, high-spirited and playful. Fiona is brainier and more unconventional than any other woman or man I have come across, and it's a challenge to keep up with her. In fact, I wonder what she sees in me. She's prettier than I am, shrewder, more talented, she has better prospects and her family seems surprisingly normal.

On the plus side for me I suppose there's the fact that I speak French. My father is a prestigious professor at the English Department and that makes heads turn when we enter the amphitheatre at college. I'm also quite tender, having had my hand held by both father and mother and siblings every night before going to bed for the first nine years of my life.

As well as this, I am definitely proficient at tickling - a much-neglected skill in the art of courting and sustaining a relationship. I cannot believe that, for all its sound advice, tickling is not even mentioned in Ovid's *Ars Amatoria*. In fact, he doesn't even make much of the eponymous arse in his title. Believe me, the answer to many a couple's conflicts can be resolved with a hearty session of tickling. In fact, when I think back, I might perhaps have made Paola fall in love with me if I had thought of tickling her at the time.

They should create tickle-parlors for stressed-out business men, for people who never laugh anymore, and another one for those who never have. Singles tickle parties, preventive tickle parties for potential divorcees, tickle queues. A good tickle will send roots shooting from your soul to the past, it will awaken the carefree fun of childhood. If you were never tickled as a child, it will put you back in touch with that quintessential thing that's missing.

A skilful tickle requires just the right amount of pressure. You also have to locate a person's favourite tickle points through trial and error until you know exactly where to go to send your partner into ecstatic laughter. Even people who intensely dislike being tickled because it makes them feel violated can learn to enjoy it through careful, judiciously monitored caress-tickling.

It is wrong to assume that statistics are right when they indicate that only 32% of the world population responds with pleasure to tickling. Those that claim to be insensitive to tickles can easily be won over and those who complain that tickling is unpleasant or even painful just aren't being tickled with enough subtlety.

If tickling doesn't do it for you, there's always the finger-in-the-arse technique. This may sound a bit coarse, and I'm sorry if I wrote that too bluntly, but it's remarkably effective. If your sex life with the same partner is drooping, looking staler every time, as it inevitably will after a while, try sticking a greased or moistened finger straight into his or her bottom, even in old age. Try it - believe me - it works. They should really give this piece of advice in marriage counsels. The mayor should mention it when newly-weds sign the register. Lawyers should ask the question before they agree to legally represent clients filing for divorce.

Thankfully, Fiona is ideally receptive to the fine art of tickling and I learn to become proficient in it with her. In case you happen to meet her, you should know that Fiona can be tickled almost indefinitely with an unflagging level of laughter and excitement. With regular breaks, so she can regain her breath and not go into overdrive, she can be kept going for hours. This method keeps our relationship afloat after the initial flurry of chemical attraction begins to settle. It generates a sense of deep-seated joy in moments when life starts to look dull, when conversation begins to slacken and sex seems repetitive. It may be artificially-induced laughter, it is joyous laughter nonetheless.

Meanwhile, our college lectures are still as exciting. We sit at the back of the amphitheatre and listen to classes on seventeenth-century poetry.

Fiona deftly masturbates me as I take lecture notes for the two of us on "To His Coy Mistress"; I fiddle with her clitoris as she takes notes on *Samson Agonistes*.

When the Associate Professor - who we later learn is divorcing her hapless husband because he caught her frolicking with the genitals of another faculty member - somewhat quaveringly and movingly recites Robert Herrick's "Corinna's Going A-Maying", Fiona discreetly beats me off to the beat of its iamb, surprisingly the ideal masturbatory rhythm.

>Come, let us go while we are in our prime
>And take the harmless folly of the time.
>>We shall grow old apace and die
>>Before we know our liberty.
>>Our life is short, and our days run
>>As fast away as does the sun;
>And, as a vapour or a drop of rain,
>Once lost, can ne'er be found again,
>>So when or you or I are made
>>A fable, song, or fleeting shade,
>>All love, all liking, all delight
>>Lies drowned with us in endless night.
>Then while time serves and we are but decaying,
>Come, my Corinna, come, let's go a-Maying.

Fiona leaves the iambic rhythm behind for a speedier, more emphatic, spondaic beat when she feels I am close to a-Moaning. Not having a tissue at hand, on the spur of the moment she reaches swiftly for the Norton Anthology of *Poetry In English*, slaps my cock down like a hotdog into the centre of Robert Herrick's famous lyric, closes the pages of the massive paperback over my throttled, throbbing member and lets me spurt out several jets of mayonnaise into the bread roll of poetry.

Of course, she has taken my copy of the fabulous anthology and by the time I get around to cleaning the mess later at home, the pages are solidly glued together and Robert Herrick's wonderful poem is forever inaccessible to me in that book.

A few days later, Fiona confides that she has been knitting a scarf for me out of a tricolor ball of Angora wool which she places within the remit of her snatch. She claims it augments the creative potential of her birthing canal and makes her feel like a spider. I watch her knit me a patriotic green, white and gold scarf in a state of barely conscious bliss.

*

Just before the Christmas holidays, one of our lecturers in the English department, a visiting professor called Peter Polysemy, makes a statement one day in the amphitheatre that spreads across the campus like wildfire and fades just as fast. It gives you an idea of the difference between America and Ireland at this time. In University College Cork, it is finally treated as nothing more than a flash in the pan, a storm in a teacup, scarcely more than a damp squib in terms of repercussions. In a PC American University, Professor Polysemy would probably have been dismissed from tenure and from office, first thing in the morning.

Nine years into the future, Philip Roth will write *The Human Stain*, a great novel about the potentially tragic consequences that lurk behind the multiple nature of many English words. In the novel, a college professor is forced to resign after he is accused of having recourse to racial language. In the course of a lecture, the unfortunate hero of Roth's novel has asked if two African American students are "spooks", meaning are they absent or present merely as ghosts. The potentially ambivalent word is misinterpreted as a racial slur.

Professor Polysemy's scandalous statement is, on the contrary, no slip of the tongue, no misinterpreted, ambiguous word. Two wimpled Nigerian nuns have been religiously attending the lecture on Anglo-Saxon Literature from the beginning of the term. When, on one occasion, one of them comes in late and unaccompanied, Professor Polysemy enquires

"Where is your friend? Have you eaten her?"

Apartheid ends in South Africa. A record solar eclipse occurs. Mike

Tyson is convicted for the rape of Miss Black America. Dublin becomes the European Capital of Culture. The Dead Sea Scrolls are made publicly available. Nadine Gordimer is awarded the Nobel Prize for Literature.

Ku Klux Klan Grand Wizard David Duke almost becomes governor of Louisiana. The first space probe lands on an asteroid. The KGB officially stops operations. The last oil well fire in Kuwait is extinguished. Freddie Mercury dies of AIDS. Frank Capra and Miles Davis check out. *The Silence of the Lambs* is in the cinemas.

22

Annus Horribilis

Dracula and *Basic Instinct* are released. George Bush vomits violently into Japanese Prime Minister Kiishi Miyazawa's lap at a state dinner. Japan apologizes for forcing Korean women into sexual slavery during WWII.

Mafia car bombs kill anti-mafia judges Falcone and Borsellino. Massacres occur in Bosnia and Herzegovina. Earthquakes in Nicaragua, Egypt and Indonesia kill thousands. The Church of England votes to allow women priests. Pope John Paul II apologizes for the mistreatment of Galileo Galilei.

The year begins auspiciously but ends somewhat disastrously for both me and Queen Elizabeth. The fire simmering beneath the surface of Fiona's calm exterior begins to fan into much larger flames. She becomes peevish and then gradually downright aggressive. Unwittingly, I must be causing her a good deal of frustration.

I cease to tickle her, not because my faith in tickling is shaken but because I no longer feel like pleasuring an ill-tempered, increasingly unfair Fiona. Nothing I do any more finds favor with her fault-finding gaze. I fail to understand her mood swings and can only surmise that I have become a bore to her. She has taken to picking her nose during our lovemaking and keeps requesting greater and greater stimuli. She asks me to slap her on the bottom until the palm of my hand feels it has been spanking a cactus.

Things begin to take a turn for the worse the day Fiona asks to perform her ithyphallic tricks in front of my eight younger brothers. She is on the cusp of becoming a confirmed performance artist and needs to practice her body art on a much wider public. Cork, she claims, has a lot of catching up to do by comparison with Feminist Art in London. It's her patriotic duty to launch nude performance art in Ireland.

At first I decline, but under persistent pestering and the threat that she will try it in Patrick Street otherwise, I agree to let her do it in front of three handpicked older brothers, Brian, Thorsten and Ian.

In the end, it's more than a little embarrassing, but worth it just to see the look on my brothers' faces. Neither of them has a girlfriend and the idea of a woman's naked body is as mysterious and inaccessible to them as the bottom of the ocean.

In the event, Brian looks as if he is about to pass out with pleasure. Thorsten's mouth releases a long string of dribble that is still tied to his lower lip when it reaches the floor. Ian has the expression of an underage boy watching *Nightmare on Elm Street*.

When Fiona asks to do it in front of my dad, however, I tell her it is out of the question. Exactly why it's out of the question, I'm not sure. Probably mostly jealousy.

It all ends unexpectedly during a casual conversation about the future and how we see it not happening together. We part on amicable terms and the break is almost painless to begin with.

After a few months, I pay a visit to Fiona's apartment. We are nervous about meeting and when Fiona takes out a bottle of whiskey it seems like a good idea.

We sit in the comfortable armchairs in the living room and drink Irish whiskey. After a whole glass each, nothing happens. We don't feel a thing so we gulp down another. When the bottle is almost empty, I get up to check how tipsy I am and at first unbelievably I am reasonably fine. I can even stand on one leg without keeling over. But then, before we realize it, the whiskey kicks in and we spend the evening attempting to drunkenly kiss, vomiting profusely on the carpet. It ends the relationship with a whimper and puts me off the smell of whiskey for life.

Nevertheless, we segue into friendship with ease. My parents are astonished at how civilised we seem. They don't know what goes on in Fiona's fiery mind. She even tells me about her new relationships and I bear it with hardly more than a tweak from the green-eyed monster. She informs me quite bluntly that she regularly bares her breasts in discotheques to the approval of all, has sex with bouncers and is teaching her flatmate's poodle to perform cunnilingus and her vagina to play the tin whistle. After being told that, I begin to wonder if Fiona is not merely a figment of my hallucinatory, overheated imagination.

When the year ends, Fiona decides to apply for a Master's degree in Trinity College Dublin. At first, she writes me letters to keep me burning up with longing. Then they peter out and we lose track of each other forever.

The impact of her absence leaves a brief crater in my life which is immediately filled in by my voluminous family, my talkative sisters and obsessive, football-minded brothers.

And just as things are getting back to normal, I meet the Irish equivalent of Calamity Jane. You must be thinking that at some unconscious level I have a craving for crazy women. Something within me must be deeply out of kilter or I wouldn't draw such amorous doom on my head. Nothing could be further from the truth, at least on a conscious level. Of course, I like a little originality in a girl, having had such an eccentric childhood, but after Fiona, I am very consciously, very cautiously looking for a standard, conventional, run-of-the-mill, common-or-garden, almost boring relationship. Someone as sensible and demure as Deirdre would be fine.

In an interview I read, Philip Roth says that he doesn't believe in psychoanalysis. He refuses to give credence to the idea that we compulsively get ourselves into dysfunctional relationships. If you are in a rotten relationship, it's just bad luck and nothing else that is driving you. Bad Luck at this point of my life is definitely in the front seat of my car and it is only much later into adult life that I meet women who are both intelligent, resourceful, sensitive, caring, alluring and non-neurotic – some of them a good deal better than me.

For the time being, I end up coming across a girl who seems both enlightened and well-balanced at first, always calm, accepting, tolerant, spontaneous but not too much, cheerful but not gung-ho, intellectual but not Heideggerian.

In a word, she looks like a wonderful choice, and for the first eight months she is, but then for the second time in my love life, all hell breaks loose. You just wonder where these things come from. Most people seem pretty normal until you spend eight months kissing and penetrating them and then it all comes out. All the neuroses and pathologies that lie dormant under the surface begin to leak out, as if penetration punches holes in a watertight, air-locked capsule that isn't supposed to be breached.

A fire breaks out in Windsor castle. Queen Elizabeth declares the year to be an *annus horribilis*, which translates best as "a horrible anus." Ireland rejects abortion. The first SMS message is sent. The Folies Bergère music hall closes its doors. Bill Clinton is elected president. Miley Cyrus sticks out her tongue for the first time. Isaac Asimov, Marlene Dietrich, Francis Bacon and Benny Hill go south.

23

Kleptomania and Urine

Czechoslovakia separates into Slovakia and the Czech Republic in what becomes known as the velvet divorce. The Russian space station Mir hosts the first art exhibition in outer space. Janet Reno becomes the first female attorney general of the United States. Several bombs explode in Bombay.

North Korea withdraws from the Nuclear Nonproliferation Treaty. South Africa officially abandons its nuclear programme. Brandon Lee dies after having been accidentally shot on the set of *The Crow*. A nuclear accident occurs in Tomsk.

Jane and I are in love. Although Jane is relatively plain, she has exquisite hands and I am still at the age in which one thinks that beautiful hands are trustworthy indicators of simplicity and goodness.

We freewheel down from winter into spring, inhaling the scent of rained-on grass and mist-filtered air. Daffodils are sprouting their colors by the roadside, cows patiently shave the ever-green Irish grass from the fields, swallows sail above us and disappear suddenly into the cracks of stone bridges, a bumble bee bangs off my forehead, midges find their way up Jane's nostrils. It's a heart-lifting day and it hasn't rained in two hours.

The English department syllabus is keeping me busy reading the highlights of Anglo-Irish literature. *Gulliver's Travels, Melmoth the Wanderer,*

The Picture of Dorian Gray, The Wild Irish Girl, At-Swim-Two-Birds, The Third Policeman, The Playboy of the Western World, Philadelphia Here I Come!, poems by Yeats, Heaney, Boland, Muldoon.

I look up to Jane because she is already a trainee history-and-math teacher in a convent school, despite the fact that she's totally irreligious and has to hide that orientation during her interview. The idea that anyone can be good at both math and a subject from the humanities blows my mind. I have infinite admiration for that kind of multidirectional brain and the way Jane moves her lips seems to express infinite hidden mysteries.

Jane's calamity eyes are blue. Her pupils are lined with miniature flames that give you the impression you are looking up into the heads of two sunflowers with the sky in the background. She has the Germanic charm of Goldilocks and it's only in later months that three massive grisly grizzly bears emerge from the surface of her character.

Before it all begins to totter and topple, however, we enjoy nights at the theatre, evenings at the Triskel Arts Centre, the Granary, the Capitol. We jangle the bells on Shandon Hill, we listen to the boys' choir in Saint Finbarr's Cathedral, we go pub-crawling, shop-licking, disco-dancing and canoeing.

We even go for a Spring swim and make love in the dangerously polluted River Lee with its average flow rate of 40.4 cubic metres per second, and come away unscathed with no skin disease, corrosive vaginal fungus or mutation of the penis.

For a while, it seems as if nothing can go wrong. Even the eventual boredom induced by routine is kept well at bay. We tell each other the stories of the books that we read and both find it's a fiery form of foreplay.

But, as Friedrich Nietzsche once said, we spend our lives swinging like a pendulum from boredom to suffering. Henry James said it in a slightly more positive way: we move from "bliss to bale" in the wink of an eye.

It all starts to go wrong one day when my mother asks if anyone has seen her voice-controlled alarm clock. None of my now twenty-three siblings has seen it and even Ian the fibber seems to be telling the truth.

Time goes by, and then my father's gold ring, the one that has lain on his bedside table for almost a decade because it's too small for his finger, goes missing. A week later, £50 goes astray from my mother's purse and then she notices that two checks have been removed from the back of the checkbook. Deirdre's diary disappears (which makes me wonder if I haven't been stealing in my sleep) and Aoife's pretty new watch is nowhere to be found.

Patrick and Cormac bemoan the loss of their horn-shaft penknives and Aine, Grainne and Frieda start crying one day because they can't find the set of ivory heirloom figurines ceded to them by our late grand-aunt.

The atmosphere at home is tense, to say the least. Table talk is reduced to hypothesizing about who the culprit is and how he or she has been able to steal from the household without getting caught. A thorough search of the house is conducted to see if none of us is stashing the loot away in some hidden recess.

Nothing is found and it's obvious there hasn't been a break-in. We all agree it has to be some kind of inside job. Cormac and Thorsten decide to try and catch the thief with a trap but Siobhan and Sif shut them up saying we're hardly going to catch the culprit if he's listening to the plan. The discussions usually end in recrimination when one or another of my siblings take to accusing each other of the theft.

The situation takes a turn for the decidedly strange when mother convenes us to the sitting room to announce that the blue and yellow Swedish vase she bought last summer contains about half a litre of urine.

"Your-in?"

"Yes, urine. Now I want to know who did that, and all the rest of it and I want to know NOW!"

"Deirdre, what's yourin?"

In the end, no one owns up and the mystery remains intact.

Five days later, there is piss in the teapot. Two days after that, one of our plants starts to yellow at the edges. The thieving seems to have stopped, but pissing has taken its place.

When one evening we hear Martin Montcocq shouting from his pile-muffled office mezzanine that we are to come here at once, he is still spitting into his Dad's Mug which he shows us with disgust has a pool of milky yellow liquid at the bottom.

"Who has been micturating in my mug?" says Daddy Bear.

He is in the habit of sipping small amounts of cold tea that is sometimes several days old, but the addition of piss is not to his liking.

Our mother decides to ground us until the perpetrator spills the beans. She is "SICK AND TIRED of this and IT BETTER NOT HAPPEN AGAIN!"

There are to be no more outings, no boyfriends, girlfriends or friends, no more fun, no more anything until this situation is cleared up and over with. I complain that I am over 18 now and technically an adult and so entitled to go out when I feel like it, but that holds no sway with mother or father who, like a lot of parents, never really manage to realise that their grown-up children should be considered as equals.

When a week has passed, no one has confessed a thing. The pissing and pilfering have stopped, but we are grounded for another week and then yet another for good measure. There are still no more desecrations, defilements, thefts or confessions, so finally mother gives in to our pressure and all things go back to normal. Friends are allowed back in and Jane and I resume our sitting room snogs on the couch.

But just after Jane leaves, I notice that the silver chain my grandmother gave me is missing from my drawer and from then onwards I begin to suspect her.

After one of our particularly vigorous brass rubbings on the couch, Jane slips off to the bathroom. I tiptoe up the stairs after a minute, to listen at the door. Not hearing a thing, I walk around to the bedrooms and hear the sound of water being trickled onto what sounds like a towel or the carpet.

The door has been left slightly ajar so I manage to lever my head into the gap without making the hinge whine, and there, to my consternation and dismay, is Calamity Jane crouching over with her back turned to the door, her perfectly rounded white buttocks spread so invitingly that Ruth Kelly's bottomous beauty pales by comparison. The trickling noise coming out of her has turned into a hiss and it's gurgling and bubbling straight into my mother's patent leather handbag.

I stand there both shocked and aroused by the sudden manifestation. This is the genuine thing - the Joycean epiphany the lecturer in Anglo-Irish studies has been talking about. It's Joycean in every possible meaning of the term, both immanent and transcendent, both odiferous and sonorous and fruitfully fleshy.

I am so astounded I scarcely know what to do, think or say. I wait and watch and stand there flummoxed, suspended in a state of horrified pleasure, weighing up the consequences, wondering if I should just leave before Jane turns around and discovers that I've been watching her.

Then it ends, the spraying comes to an abrupt stop, and I am seconds away from causing her to be caught in what I still believe will be the most humiliating moment in her life.

She wiggles her posterior a little up and down and then, instead of getting up, starts to undulate so becomingly I can feel a boner rising up irresistibly.

"Did you like that, dirty boy?"

"-?"

"I said, did you enjoy it?"

"Did you know I was watching you?"

"I knew you were bound to follow me at some point. You took a while to cotton on, though. The last family I did this to had me sussed out in less than two weeks."

"What are you saying? Could you at least turn round and face me?"

"I'm saying it's taken you ages to suspect me and I just love your consternation."

"How could you - ? How could you do this?"

"It's in my nature."

"Please stop trying to sound so cool. I don't believe you're half as detached as you sound."

"I do love you. It's just I can't help doing this sort of thing. I need the excitement, and you're a pretty straightforward sort of nice guy."

"Aren't OCDs when you need to wash your hands forty times a day or lock and unlock the door three times in a row or avoid all the cracks in the footpath? I have some myself. Stealing objects from your boyfriend's house and pissing in his mother's fucking handbag is a little bit different."

"Kleptomania isn't an OCD. It's an ICD. Impulse Control Disorder."

"I see, so you're a kleptomaniac now. When were you actually thinking of letting me know about all this? On our wedding night?"

"Oh, come on, we aren't anywhere near marriage! You haven't even given me a ring. Anyway, I've let you know now, haven't I? I wasn't exactly discreet about nicking, or pissing. You could have caught me dozens of times. It's a wonder I wasn't caught earlier, what with all your siblings coming and going. You aren't exactly Mr Quick on the Uptake, but you're sweet."

"What am I going to tell my parents? Sorry Mum, Jane pissed in your favourite handbag but she didn't really mean to. It was really just an impulse. Don't take it personally. You'll get used to the smell. I mean - Do you have other O or ICDs you'd like to mention now that we're on the topic?"

"None I want to talk about just now."

"Stop making me feel like I'm interrogating a defenceless damsel in distress. Would you mind standing up and putting your trousers on? You do know this is my parents' room and either of them could walk in here any second. What am I supposed to tell them? *Oh sorry, Jane thought she was in the toilet.*"

"Darling, you shouldn't get so angry. I know this is a bit surprising and all, but think of it as a kind of love test. If you get over this, it means you really love me. My last boyfriend. Kevin. I told you about him. Well, he was so furious he wanted his mother to call the police, and the guy before that, Jonathan. He actually tried to tie me up till his parents got home. I mean, what kind of love is that? I left them on the spot."

"So, you've done this how many times? Is this like some rite of passage you expect me to endure? Haven't I told you that I've already had to cope with Fiona? She caused me enough heartache for a lifetime. Jesus, why do I get the crazy ones? Talk about the sufferings of Job! I mean of all the normal, balanced women out there, I have to get all the whacky - Sorry, I didn't mean to say it that way, it's just - I've been through this already and it just - it killed me. I feel mentally damaged."

"I know. I can't help it. I've always had this and probably always will so if you want to stay with me, you'll have to deal with it."

"Isn't there treatment for this? Have you been to see a doctor?"

"Of course I have. And I have medicine. Mood stabilizers and inhibitors, only they don't agree with me. I get nauseous so I usually don't take them."

The conversation ends with some hugging and kissing but it just isn't the same after that and the more she sees my doubts the harder she makes it for me to forgive her even though I know it's not her fault. The worst part is that she never really says sorry for any of it and just expects me to take it for granted, like an addiction to sugar.

Our parents have always reared us to adapt and make allowances for cultural relativism and tolerance and so on but I just can't take the casualness and sense of entitlement Jane adopts whenever the question comes up in conversation. And I can't help feeling betrayal sitting deep in my chest.

In the later stages of our breakup, sensing she is about to lose me, Jane resorts to more desperate attempts to force me to keep her. She rails and derails, throws my bag out the window, tears up my books, rips my clothes with her teeth, pretends to have lost the faculty of speech, steals from my pocket. She threatens me with scissors, a hefty-bladed kitchen knife, opens the car door while I'm driving and tries to cross the dual carriageway during rush hour. She threatens to set fire to my parents' house and then her own apartment.

I realize that if guns were allowed in Ireland she would probably already have shot me or at least trained a gun on my face, so I decide to find a way of leaving her without it all ending horribly.

The key to making this happen smoothly, of giving her the impression that she is not being let down, is to give her the sense that she is leaving me and not the opposite. It's cowardly enough, I know, and I never really forgive myself, but she's more than I can take.

I long, and realize I have always longed for what Virginia Woolf wanted for herself and for individuals in general, a room of my own, a place I can just be silent in, a place that shuts out the clamor, the cries and the knocks, the talking and complaining, the grappling and wrangling. Just to sit inside a diamond of the first water and experience the soundlessness at the heart of it. Nothing else. Just that pure carat silence.

What I do in the event is simple enough. I gently push poor painful Jane into someone else's arms.

Let me make it clear that I do not palm her off onto another hapless bloke who will end up palely loitering as she pisses into his mother's handbag. I make her be unfaithful to me by calling up my hunkiest friends from the past and the present. I even get in touch with Robert Smith from primary school. He is not as handsome as I remember him but he is still a good deal above average and happy to oblige.

The idea is kind of horrible, I'll admit it, but in the circumstances, it's all I can do to save myself, and in the end, it also saves Jane. In the event, she falls out of love with me and doesn't fall in love with any of them straight away, and that's precisely the point. I want her to feel the relativity of all partners again so that she lets go of her attachment.

The power of sex does its work. It slowly weans her off me, reminding her that fulfilling sex and tenderness can be obtained from more than a few able-bodied Irish youths. I finally break it off with her when she is just about to leave for her parents' place in Donegal.

She goes home to sob in her father's arms and then phones up Jerry Joyce and later Robert Smith and asks them to come up and see her. I beseech them to go up together, pay for their car rental and tell them to take her on a drive to the Giant's Causeway to put things in perspective.

It goes off swimmingly and the three of them end up building a *ménage à trois* that lasts for seven years until Robert leaves for another man and Jane and Jerry head for the altar. Last news I hear, her O and ICDs are down to being a battle axe at the office and harboring a few finicky obsessions in the home, having her husband wash all the dishes twice in a row and making him iron the children's underpants, socks and handkerchiefs. It's the politically correct nineties and Jerry loves his children so he puts up with his surprisingly enterprising wife.

*

The whole family is woken up one peaceful spring night, howling and sweating. An ear-shattering clap of thunder accompanied by a blinding flash of lightning has just exploded from under us in the sitting room.

In the wake of the blast, the whole house shudders and groans on its joists. Lightbulbs and windows have shattered. Bits of cough-inducing ceiling collapse onto our beds and the wall-to-wall carpet. Part of the paintwork and plaster on the wall of our room collapses revealing hidden clods of Seamus Heaney Heritage Peat™, ribbed and strengthened by the tannin-preserved bones that our parents have used to insulate the house. The entire family rushes out, clogging the corridor.

Ian, Siofra and Samuel have their hands in their plaster-rimmed mouths. Una, Sophia, Aoife, Emil, Patrick, Søren, Siobhan, Frieda, Anna, Áine, Gráinne, Colm and Cormac are screeching and crying and whining in various degrees of distress. The babies are squalling and howling in a chorus of terror. Our parents emerge from their bedroom looking wild-eyed and shell-shocked.

Martin, Deirdre, Sif, Brian, Thorsten, Owen, Liam, Diarmuid and I make our way cautiously down the carpeted, powdered, debris-strewn stairs. Using a knitted hat as a glove, we try to push the steaming hot handle of the sitting room door, but it remains stubbornly shut.

Martin Montcocq rams the door in masterfully with his shoulder and the timber gives way with a crunchy cracking sound. The rectangle of wood swings inwards, creaks and collapses off its hinges.

The spectacle we witness leaves us open-mouthed and speechless.

The entire sitting room is a black bombed out shelter. The walls and the ceiling are scorched and singed. Mother's Persian rug has been projected to the wall and looks like a burnt piece of toast. The table lies shattered and splayed. The smell of something like ancient gunpowder pokes acridly up into the nostrils. Every object, including the chairs, is either burnt to a cinder, melted, smoking, or split into fragments. Most objects have fled to the corners of the room.

The windows are all missing and a breeze is blowing in. Books, glass, planks, papers, radios, reading lamps, maps, shards of porcelain and vinyl records, Catholic knick-knacks of all manner and kind lie strewn over the garden. The books that are still on the fractured bookshelves in the room are burnt black and frazzled.

The piano has caved in and looks like the inside walls of a chimney. The music rack and the lid have entirely disappeared and the teeth of the keyboard are all black and broken. There isn't a single white key left to the view. Even the hole drilled by Brian in the middle C is covered in a thick layer of soot.

Embedded in the burnt woodwork of the collapsed fall board above the keys is a shattered metal object that looks strangely like the exploded remains of the brass heirloom candlestick which Martin Montcocq inherited from his father, the one which had the mysteriously sealed heavy chamber at the bottom, the one we sing to for birthdays and our *Excellentes Soirées*. Martin remembers that he forgot to blow out the candle in the candlestick before going to bed.

In silence, his hand gloved in the knitted woollen hat, he tugs out what's left of the candlestick from where it is wedged in the piano, cradling the still steaming object in the crook of his arm. He looks us in the eye with an air of relief, and declares World War II finally over.

Eritrea gains independence from Ethiopia. Kim Campbell becomes the first female prime minister of Canada. Lorena Bobbitt cuts off her husband's penis.

Father Pino is assassinated outside his church on his birthday for his anti-mafia activity. An earthquake in India kills over 10,000 people. The Sri Lankan civil war begins.

In the Downing Street Declaration, the British government commits itself to finding a solution to the problem of Northern Ireland. A mob sets fire to the Turkish hotel where Aziz Nesin, the translator of *The Satanic Verses*, is residing, killing 37 people. Audrey Hepburn and Federico Fellini expire.

24

The Ship of Death

The Zapatista army begins the war in Mexico. Boris Yeltsin and Bill Clinton decide to deactivate missiles aimed at Russia and America. The Northridge earthquake leaves 26,000 homeless. Clinton calls for a ban on assault weapons. A man fires two blank shots at Prince Charles in Australia. *Four Weddings and a Funeral* and *Interview with a Vampire* are released. *Pulp Fiction* and *In the Name of the Father* receive prizes.

Edward Munch's *The Scream* is stolen in Oslo and the Winter Olympics begin in Lillehammer. The Rwandan massacre of Tutsis begins. South Africa holds its first multiracial elections.

Having survived an explosion that could have wiped our entire family out, I finish my Masters dissertation on the poetry of Derek Walcott, get the degree with a surprisingly good mark, despite the fact that my dissertation is, objectively speaking, often fanciful, inaccurate and pretentiously written in high-flown, overblown, sub-academic prose. This is Ireland and marks are generous. External examiners, even the British ones, are lenient and magnanimous. It's the Hiberno-Saxon world and bad marks have been pin-marked as bad for the person, detrimental to society.

My feelings of shell-shocked trauma and amorous betrayal slosh around like dirty brown bathwater in my brain. Thoughts of Jane become entangled with thoughts of Disaster and Dissertation in a defeating synaptic maelstrom. By the end of the year, I've read so many articles, gargled so much jargon, that there's a knot in my tongue and a crumpling in my soul.

The possibility of going to Oxford to write a PhD has opened up, despite my half-hearted attempts to contact the various Oxbridge colleges and solicit scholarships. No grants come my way, but a kindly professor from New College invites me to come over and talk in his leather-swathed, fire-placed, marble-arched, Persian-carpeted office.

One of my grandmothers is willing to pay the exorbitant fees required for entry to this second Academic Eden, but my heart isn't in it. The thought of spending another four years juggling the jargon appeals to me about as much as spending four years in a coffin with a food and air supply, mildew and bookworms testing my flesh.

I need to live and get a change of scenery. I have a strong attraction for all things British, probably because in the end there is next to no anti-Brit sentiment voiced by the people I know, and *Faulty Towers* is still very popular in Ireland. I have an immoderate fondness for Britons that I cannot quite explain. The feeling is anything but PC from an Irish perspective and I know many an Irish youth who would punch my lights out for saying what I'm about to confess.

I think that the bullying that my brothers and I have had to put up with in secondary school at the hands of borderline psychotic Irish teenagers makes me semi-consciously feel that the Irish in general deserve the treatment meted out to them by the English.

Of course, I realize that bullying in English schools is just as ferocious as in Ireland and that the English also deserve to be colonized and punitively sodomized by the Irish.

My feeling in those days is that Ireland is less like a distinct country than a borough, the westernmost part of England, despite seventy years of independence. Our coins are modelled on the English ones, our double-decker buses have the same shape with a different color, we speak an only slightly greener version of English, our chocolates and sweets are the same to the extent that Una and Ian firmly believe that Cadbury is an

Irish company which makes guaranteed Irish chocolate. Our shops look the same, our food is the same, our fuck-you sign language is the same, even our footpaths are the same and - this is ultimately why I don't leave for England - English rain is fundamentally very close in spirit and quantity to the Irish variety. I've had so much rain since birth it sometimes feels I'm still not out of the amniotic sack.

At other times, England feels like Eastern Ireland. You go to visit your cousin in Liverpool, your little sister goes to get an abortion in County England. County America is a place you can visit when you switch on the television.

In the end, although part of me yearns to fathom the eccentric and exotic depths of the English soul as something distinct and intriguing, I decide to head for much sunnier climes. There are lots of destinations to choose from, but Italy and Greece only appeal to me as holiday locations, so I decide, after having read Orwell's *Down and Out in Paris and London* to head for the French capital to try and make it as a writer.

I haven't managed to write much in the Montcocq noise-hold, just a few desultory short stories, two attempts at a novel, one in English, one in French, but the idea of roughing it, spending my day writing in the *Café de Flore*, sleeping on top of a high-rise at night - hopefully the Tour Montparnasse - has got me in thrall. If I'm unable to gain access to the roof of a skyscraper (there aren't many to choose from in Paris), I've decided to sleep under a bridge. An ivory tower writer or a guttersnipe. Or maybe a bit of the two.

The thought of sleeping outside in the company of a few tramps, pimps and prostitutes seems convivial, safe and quiet after having been subjected to the noise pollution of the household. I'm such a gullible, guileless greenhorn that the notion of real danger doesn't even pass through my mind. What I like is the idea that by facing the moon on a high-rise rooftop or bivouacking under a bridge I am - though not in literary terms at least in existential terms - out-orwelling Orwell who slept in the dosshouse with at least the creature comfort of a roof over his head.

I have a sum of money tucked away in a bank account, and a visa card with which to withdraw it in small amounts so I won't have money stolen from me at night. My father has given me much sensible advice and bought me the latest high-tech Swedish sleeping bag designed to withstand the howling cold winds of the North. He is proud that I've decided to camp rough again and sleep on the banks of the Seine if I have to for the sake of thrift and what he calls "derring-do" (which to my poor worried-sick mother means absolute recklessness, despite the fact that she has done this kind of thing herself more than once during her pregnant cycling trips).

The magic of writing in the same cafés as Joyce, Fitzgerald, Hemingway, Stein, Orwell, De Beauvoir and Sartre is so overwhelming it pushes me to tell the family that I've decided to make the move. The dismay on most of their faces is so patent that for a few weeks I relent and let the idea stagnate, but I long to fly by the nets of Ireland which I feel are holding my Joycean spirit down.

The worst snares I fall foul of are really just rain nets cast down from the sky almost every day, but I'm so sick of rain I feel like a climatic refugee in search of solar asylum.

And yet, before I leave, I am startled into thinking that the other Irish nets so powerfully evoked by Joyce and Patrick Kavanagh can actually be broken.

RTE 1 unexpectedly broadcasts footage of a Brazilian crowd celebrating their fourth victory at the World Cup. Up to then, the image I have of Brazil is limited to what I have learnt in Geography class. I see it as a vast jungle full of parrots and anacondas and blowgun shooting shrub-dwellers. I know there are cities of course but they just don't seem real. The footage shown on our brand-new television displays a throng of enthusiasts so deliriously happy they're practically eating their flag. They chant, scream with joy, laugh like nothing I've ever seen in Ireland or abroad. They dance, jostle, sing like there's no more tomorrow. And then suddenly, I see something that seems unimaginable - impossible - on Irish television.

A buxom Brazilian beauty pushes through the crowd, addresses the camera suggestively and peels up her T-shirt to reveal the most staggeringly beautiful, braless brown breasts I am capable of imagining.

The Pleasures of Queueing

I just can't believe that this is happening on Irish TV. And yet there they are, those lovely appendages, lolling and lilting in the Brazilian heat. Imprinted all over the feverish footage of Irish telly by a cameraman no doubt in a state of prolonged erogenous seizure.

I watch the swaying flesh magic for seconds that seem suspended in time, and then before you know it, the breasts are gone from Irish television for ever. But their languorous loitering abides with us here in Ireland, remaining as an antidote for climatic depression, boosting public morale for over a year. World-cup breasts. Every Irishman imagines himself cradled and nursed by them, cuddled and mollycoddled by those soft, hard-nippled wonders. Along with two million other Irishmen, I nuzzle and worry them as I lie sleepless in bed. I bury my face in their pillows. We surround them and feed off them like a cloud of Irish midges.

This cloudburst in the history of Irish television is soon covered over for me, however, when I learn that a hapless RTE weather forecaster has just been suspended three months for releasing some of his meterological frustration by announcing one day to fellow-suffering Irish spectators nationwide that "we're in for some *shitty* weather yet again".

In the early 1990s, a University professor who insinuates that Africans are barbaric is exonerated, but a forecaster who impugns the quality and character of Irish weather is suspended on the spot.

The poor guy has probably been dying to pronounce the word *shitty* since he got the job. Can you imagine the frustration of having to announce Irish weather? Rain, rain, rain. Grisly drizzly. Rain in small quantities, rain in large quantities. Rain that needles your skin and your spirit, rain that bounces back up into your face. Fine-grained rain, bead-curtains of rain, prison-bars of rain. Rain for breakfast, rain for dinner. Rain at night, rain in the morning, rain at dusk, rain in the afternoon. Darkness at noon, greyness at dawn. Rain for autumn, rain for winter, rain for spring. Even rain for summer. Rain in your tea, rain on your sandwiches, rain in your soup, rain in your gravy, rain in your porridge, rain in your toilet. Rain in your bed.

Yet another example of anti-Joycean parochialism clinches my decision to leave the evergreen Emerald Isle. A few weeks after the suspension of the RTE rainman, my father gives his students a text in which an art critic writes of what he calls the "gesticulating Madonnas" in Italian mannerist paintings.

Several Irish parents actually complain of indecency to the University President who goes out of his way to summon Martin Montcocq to the thick mahogany desk of his oak-panelled office.

I ask you, where is the residue of Joyce's tutelary spirit in my grenade-defeated father's hour of need? Where are the leftovers of Joyce's ghostly bones when my father is forced to apologise in front of a thick mahogany desk and then to an amphitheatre of students who know more about Madonna's hit-singles than the spiritual gestures of the Virgin Mary in Late Renaissance painting?

At that juncture, in that flashpoint, it feels like the broad nets of Ireland are falling in droves from the Skynet.

I decide to go into town the next day to buy a ferry ticket to France.

Although I will miss Ireland, I know the time is ripe, it is the only possible decision for me to make at this point. I even have a recurring dream that makes it clear that I also need to leave the family super-hive. Although I'm attached to every one of my siblings - even the latest baby twins I hardly know and whose names I keep forgetting - I can't help feeling more claustrophobia, a little bit more of it with every new arrival.

In my reiterating dream, my parents have bought a plot of land on one of the Aran Islands. They tell us that the new house is situated on the tiny plateau of a craggy cliff far above the sea. When we make our way out there for Easter, we find that our parents' plot of cliff is actually so small that there is only room for a double bed on it. Our parents haven't had enough savings to build a house yet so it's just the bare bed on the cliff top and we all have to fit in.

The space around the bed is minimal and I'm terrified of falling off the bed and the cliff. The waves are pelting the foot of the cliff like dynamite explosions. My siblings, however, don't seem to mind. They're happy and screaming and totally oblivious to the danger. They're all caught up in the fun of climbing over our parents and trading places on the bed. Even Deirdre is jumping and frolicking, totally out of character.

I finally decide to sleep at the foot of the bed on the turf which is actually just as dangerous but it feels a little bit safer and there's less of a chance that I will roll off the cliff onto the sharp rocks far below.

Admittedly, I'm pretty egocentric in this dream and don't seem to give a rat's ass about the possibility that the others might roll off too. It's nothing more than a survival fantasy, but it shows I'm not made for being a member of an insanely large family. If some of the names in this book seem to belong to characters that are insufficiently rounded, characters that fail to stand out on the page, it's because in these last few years especially there are some of my siblings that I hardly know from Adam. Even I have trouble keeping track of their names. They just run past me screaming and jostling and hankering for fun and I think which one is that? I'm sure that some of them hardly realize I'm their oldest brother.

My parents are sweet and in Winnicott terms, better than good enough parents, despite their over-enthusiastic reproductive organs, despite their war-induced thriftiness, their tandem eccentricities, the unconscionable strangeness of their quirks. And yet I still need to leave them and their anarchically noisy, unbearably overcrowded, hive-humming, head-hammering household.

If you think about it, there are at least six main categories of parent. If you attempt to fit my parents into one of the following types, you realize that I've been pretty lucky on the scale that goes from terrible to terrific.

Type 1: The parent who needs to drag you down. Let us call this variety the Cannibal parent.

Type 2: The control freak who attempts to dissolve you in his/her own personality. Let us call this kind Agent Smith.

Type 3: The parent who cannot abide your individuality and tries to break you like a pair of shoes or make minced meat out of the thing you call your self. I call this kind Agent Smithereens.

Type 4: This kind generally supports your endeavors, but secretly hopes you won't succeed better than they have. Let us call this parental model the Well-Intentioned Colossus with Feet of Clay.

Type 5: The parent who is deliriously happy that his child has achieved success, but can't help the afterthought that they didn't do quite as well as you. Let us call this one the Maenad of Love with an Afterthought.

Type 6: This is the ideal firm and loving, shoulder-carrying kind. Let us call this rare paragon of virtue Saint Christopher.

Even I am not quite sure where I would situate my parents on the scale, but all in all, they fare pretty well, despite eccentricities and post-war strictures. Probably, most parents slide from one category to another depending on the time of day, the irritability factor, how objectively unbearable the child is, etcetera.

*

Three weeks later, I am out in Cork Harbour, one of the largest natural harbors in the world. Ireland is a very small country with a wide-open exit that you can freely avail of when you feel that its rain-bars are becoming too much of a prison.

I am waving from the deck to my tearful cheerful family all lined up on the quay. Everyone has come, packed into a van and two cars. Those who couldn't find a seat have taken the bus. Everyone is waving and shouting and jumping, even the babies in arms. They look like an endlessly capacious series of Russian dolls placed side by side.

When Martin Montcocq gets home he goes to my former room and weeps. Anne Montcocq, Emil, Sammy and the girls make tea and raisin-studded scones and they all talk about how strange it feels now that the biggest brother is gone.

Swaying inside my ferry, I'm a little lachrymose too for a while, but mostly exhilarated until seasickness kicks in. Lord Byron once said that even love does not survive being sick at sea.

The ferry is practically empty, all holiday goers having returned in late August. I roam around the decks watching the landmass recede. The hum of the engines and the creaking of the boat as it rolls and surges is soothing after all those years of enduring the shouting and cheering of my rugby-team family. No more queueing in front of the bathroom, no more waiting your turn at the breakfast table, no more hanging out 25 shirts on the clothesline, no more doing the dishes for 25 people. From now on, it's just one shirt, one pants, one jumper, one underpants, one pair of socks. I have scarcely more than this in my rucksack. Just a toothbrush, toothpaste, an extra pair of shoes and socks in case it rains, an extra-resistant pair of rechargeable underpants in case the first one gets dirty, a novel by Iris Murdoch in case I get lovelorn, a novel by Angela Carter in case I get bored, two solid notebooks, some pencils, an eraser and a box of condoms which my maternal grandfather, in a state of embarrassed agitation, has bestowed upon me in the prophylactic hope that I will not return with "wan uh dose French vnaireal diseases".

After lugging my rucksack into the safety deposit locker room, I walk around along the empty corridors. The ship leans to the side and there is nothing but sea and sky and more sea. It feels like I'm in a giant, carpeted, corridored, portholed womb. A uterus fully equipped with duty-free shops, cafeterias, cinemas, showers, saunas and information desk.

My first extended stay in Anne Montcocq's womb had no information desk and was finally a little cramped for room, though I loved to lean my head against her pelvic bone. In fact, I still love to lean the weight of my forehead against a wall when times are hard. The tremendous advantage of locomotion in my mother's uterus was that I was never sea-sick inside it.

The increasing rolling motion of the ferry is getting the better of my stomach and after less than an hour I have to sit and then lie down in the lounge where I laze like a vegetable for hours, feeling weaker and more somnolent than a foetus, until the passengers begin to emerge for dinner.

I let them come and go and then decide to head for the now almost empty cafeteria. My nausea clears up after I've eaten and taken two seasick tablets so I decide to go for a swim and stay a few minutes in the sauna.

When I finally find my way round the circling corridors to the health centre, as if it's at the heart of Dante's inferno, there's no one in the pool but I hear muffled talking in the sauna.

After a quick dip in the semi-clean swimming pool, I take my swimming togs off in the showers and lace a modest towel around my waist. Although I'm technically no longer in Ireland, we're probably still in Irish waters and the boat, staff and passengers are mostly Irish so extra-decent attire obtains.

I wrench open the thick wooden door of the sauna and the humidity-laden air embraces my skin, burning my nostrils as I breathe. It's been a long time since that experience at the *bastu* when our parents took us to Sweden for the summer. The ground is hellishly hot and I quickly scamper up on to the slats.

The sauna is unbelievably large and dim. Beclouded, steamed up air makes it hard to see anything more than figures. I move gingerly towards the sound of voices at the back. The steam seems unnaturally dense, almost like fog.

As I get closer, I make out a half dozen men and some women. This is obviously a gender-neutral, co-educational sauna. I'm not sure how many women there are as everybody's naked (except me) and I'm too embarrassed to take a discreet look at their bodies for the moment.

I sit down, not listening attentively to the conversation yet, and sneak a quick glance at the men. A few of them look uncannily familiar. There are two on the very top tier of the sauna, an altitude that is almost impossible to stay on for more than a few seconds, the temperature is so hot.

They are sitting up there almost touching, practically sizzling like fried, sweating lizards, their heat-dilated Johnsons stretching out in front of them like elephantine extensions.

One of them has a thick white beard and a muss of coiling grey walrus hair on his chest. He's got a grandfatherly American accent and a throaty virile laugh. He looks like a matador at rest. The other one has a black eye patch and slicked-back hair and is clucking and nodding cheerfully to himself as he examines his fingernails.

Directly below them is a man whose face is a map-work of wrinkles. There's actually something very familiar about him too. That wizened birdy intelligent look. Could that possibly be Samuel Beckett in his birthday suit?

I take a fleeting look at the women. There's something almost pre-Victorian about one of them, despite the fact that she's also stark naked, and the other one has a slightly Puritan manner about her as if she is sitting straitlaced at a worldly dinner and is worried about her manners. I notice she sports no pubic hair and has those large, slightly puffy haloes around her nipples that I find immensely fetching.

Beside her, lying on her back, is a long-nosed, delicately-featured lady with black hair, and further down a scrawnier, lankier man with a stretched out, Adam-appled neck. He looks like George Orwell, without the toothbrush moustache. A tier below him is a thin-lipped, slit-eyed man in his seventies with balls almost the size of ostrich eggs.

Slightly apart from the group are two younger men, a heavily-bearded one in his forties, the other in his late thirties, bald and clean-shaven with a dangerous-looking tattoo at the base of his throat. I pretend not to listen to their conversation.

"You know he was able to smuggle in some ambrosia last week. Ernie and I actually managed to dry it. So we broke it up into crumbs and smoked it on deck. There we were, enjoying the "huge and birdless silence", as Philip likes to put it, smoking the food of the gods. Pretty damned good stuff to inhale. You can see why they like it. He says he can bring us some more in a fortnight."

"Oh, you boys are just too much! What if he gets caught? You know his liver is getting weaker."

"Come on, Jane, loosen up, I thought you were learning to be modern!"

"You know very well there is only so much modernity I can tolerate. It's easy for you, being young at the height of the Roaring Twenties and all. I don't think you realise how difficult it is for me to sit here in complete nudity in the company of several gentlemen, despite all the most edifying conversations I have had with David and Henry. You lost generation people take everything for granted."

"Jesus, Jane, what's a little skin display between cronies? I've noticed you still can't look at my pecker without blushing. Franz finds it hilarious. He says he saw you leaving the showers the other day as if you'd had to scrub yourself with a cockroach!"

"Really? I'm sure you find it very funny. Perhaps we should switch the rules around and we could try living in the 1780s. See how you'd like trying to fit into one of my childhood dresses. I'm sure you'd look lovely with a frilly bonnet on your pate. What do you think, Emily?"

"Oh, I'm sure he'd look 'sexy'. We should add tippet and tulle!"

"We should dress David up in ladies' clothes too. He'd look a real darling, I'm sure! Why don't you shave that beard off? It's so smelly and it makes you look like a fungus. Look how youthful George is looking since he shaved off that dreadful Hitler moustache."

"Please don't call it that, Virginia, you know how much I hate that animal. Alright, that - man. And one of my reasons for shaving it off is I wouldn't have to hear you say that any longer."

"You shouldn't hate him that much. I went down to see him the other day and he's much improved. The pain treatment has taught him to be humble so they've lowered the doses he told me. He spends his afternoons talking about his father with Sigmund and Carl and then he gets a three-hour deep massage session. They try that in Finnish prisons nowadays which is why they're trying it on him. I read an article about it. Massaging the prisoners every day, you know, so practically none of them reoffend. Anyway, he even plays chess with Maryan Maryan and Felix Nussbaum in the evenings for penance and I can tell you Maryan is giving him a hard time. When Adolf loses, which is every time, he has him sit for hours in the same position while he paints him in the most hideous shapes and colors. Says he's trying to get him to understand decadent art."

"Maybe we should do some explaining here, young man. You're looking as if you've just walked into an assembly of vampires. Don't worry, we know what you're feeling. Listen, I'm Ernest Hemingway, this is Samuel Beckett and this is James Joyce. You probably recognised them already, right? Being a Paddy and all. What's wrong? Cat got your tongue?"

"Am I ... dreaming, right now? This is a lucid dream or something, right?"

"Ahm, let's see, technically, we're not sure what to call it. What you're experiencing sometimes happens with people who have a strong spiritual connection to the arts. Don't ask me why it happens though. And don't worry, it doesn't mean you're dead or anything. You should get back to your old life. I'm pretty sure you will. Probably as soon as we leave."

"So, where am I? Is this - the Greek Underworld?"

"Hmm, that's a good guess, actually. We've changed it quite a lot though so it's rather far from what we started off with. The updated Underworld scenario was James's idea but then we got a bit bored. It was fun and first, you know, running around the corridors trying to catch the nymphs, checking out on the muses, all that. But it just felt too familiar after a while so we decided to change the sets and all. We now have theme-based settings or else we decide on who's going to imagine the decor for the week. They let us do practically anything we like. This week we're experiencing a cruise across the Irish sea, designed by D. H. Lawrence and Philip Larkin. We've called it the Ship-of-Death pleasure cruise. That probably sounds a bit chilling to you, I guess, but you've gotta understand that in this place death has none of those unpleasant connotations it has when you're alive. Everyone here is so relieved to be dead, you know. I mean, being dead is the best thing that happened to me. Ok, sometimes, I miss the excitement of war and shooting white elephants and all, and yeah, I feel a bit guilty about that. But all the suffering and conflict is gone, and, you know, it's just plain sailing. We've got everything we need here, and if anyone feels a craving for something we haven't got, then we just sit down together and try to come up with that new thing that the person is hankering for. You'll see, you'll like it here when you come to stay for good. So what is it you do? You must love lidrachure in a big way, right, cos otherwise you wouldn't be here with us."

"Well, yes, actually, I'm heading for Paris right now. Well, Roscoff first obviously, then I'm going to walk from Brittany to Paris. Maybe hitchhike. I'll see how it goes. The plan is to stay in Paris until I've finished writing a novel, sleeping by the river at night or on the top of a building if I can get up there and writing by day. I hope to have finished before the cold sets in."

"Good man yerself. I'm glad ta see that there are still youngflaz willin ta brave de torny pat ta litratchur! See fellas, he's followin in de master's footsteps. Good lad yerself. More power to yer elbow! So tell us, what do ya write about?"

"Well, it's mostly semi-autobiographical stuff, actually."

"Good, you're dead right dare, boy. Write what you know bout and you won't get outa yer dept. If ya know more about yer belly button dan you do about de lady next door, den write a novel bout yer navel."

"I don't really agree with James on that, actually. Look at me, I read 350 books about Indians in the nineteenth century so I could write about them. And I almost won the Pulitzer with it."

"Pulitzer, Schmulitzer. Prizes are a lotta gobshite and you know it! Next you'll be telling me that de Nobel prize is wurt more den de money dey give ya. Don't mind him, stick ta what you know and what you're about ta do when ya get ta Paris is my honest and truthful advice."

"Have you had any luck publishing yet? I remember having a difficult time with that. Even Samuel here had to resort to vanity publishing to begin with. Lots of us had to in fact. Emily didn't even publish at all. Are you what they call experimental?"

"Well, I'm not radically postmodern or anything, but I like to challenge the standards of the gentility principle. I'm into breaking taboos mainly. And I rather like the idea of trying to make the main character, or even the narrator into somebody who's not particularly likeable. I've been writing a kind of parody of a family chronicle."

"Sounds like a good start, what do you think, Sam? Sam? Oh, never mind him. He's in his taciturn phase again. It's so rude! God, it's hot in here. I think I'm going to go. Are you all coming? Ernest, honest to God, I don't know how you can stand sitting on the top terrace. You're frying like a sausage! Is this still about showing what a man you are?"

"Go back to sleep, Virginia. You don't know the first thing about men."

"Well, good luck to you then! We're off to a conference being given by Nadine Gordimer, Doris Lessing and André Brink on the future of the South African novel. We're quite excited about it. We like to keep up with the times, see what's being written nowadays. André Brink still has his finger on the pulse of the year."

"Aren't they still alive?"

"Well in 1994 they are, but you seem to be forgetting that we're all in a novel that's being written by you in 2017."

"Dead right - I keep forgetting that myself."

"Enjoy your time in Paris, and we'll see you soon! Even if you don't make it as a writer. We regularly have invited audiences. You just have to apply. There's room for everyone. Glad to see you attempting to walk in our footsteps. *Down and Out*, eh, I had a lot of fun writing that one. Henry Miller suggested the other day I should have called it *Down and Up*. I told him he should have called his trilogy *In and Out*."

"Good luck to ya, lad. Take it easy. And remember, silence, exile and cunning. De true writer is a god paring his fingernails."

"Don't listen to that pretentious waffle, man. Writing is about grace under pressure and keeping an iceberg in your head."

"Or an icicle in your heart."

"And remember, good taste is the enemy of creativity."

The way I see it is you have to take risks in your style or your subject matter, preferably in both. Without risk, there's no greatness."

"Forget realism. Authenticity is overrated."

"Just read, read, read your eyes out."

"Don't just read. Experience things. Go see some whores, catch a minor venereal disease, get roughed up by a pimp, try swimming in the Seine. Fall in love with more than one person at the same time, let them batter your heart. Climb a mountain, fly a Cessna into Moscow. Go to India."

"Remember, the most negative novel in the world is a very positive thing to have done."

"There are no negative experiences for the writer. Everything can be transmuted into gain."

"Don't forget to write about sex. D. H. Lawrence keeps complaining that novels these days are becoming progressively more PG."

"If at first you don't succeed, try, try again."

"Try again, fail again. Fail better."

"Thanks for the advice. I feel like such a greenhorn with all of you here."

"Don't mention it. We know what it's like to be young, and we know what it's like to be dead. Just don't take life too seriously is my final advice. Think of it as a pleasant form of Purgatory."

The Celtic Tiger kicks in just as I leave Ireland. The Channel Tunnel opens to the public. A civil war breaks out in Yemen. The Russian army leaves Estonia and Latvia. Iraq redeploys troops on the border with Kuwait. Ronald Reagan announces he has Alzheimer's.

The Australian government agrees to compensate indigenous inhabitants who were displaced during nuclear tests in the 1950s and 60s. Kim II Sung, Burt Lancaster, Jacqueline Kennedy Onassis, Richard Nixon, Kurt Cobain and Melina Mercouri evanesce. A fragment of comet Shoemaker-Levy hits Jupiter.